YN ÔL I BS/STORFA

A Guide to the Sunday Trading A...

A Guide to the Sunday Trading Act 1994

Tony Askham,
Senior Partner, Hepherd Winstanley and Pugh, Southampton
and Director of Euroshop

Butterworths
London, Dublin, Edinburgh
1994

United Kingdom	Butterworth & Co (Publishers) Ltd, Halsbury House, 35 Chancery Lane, LONDON WC2A 1EL and 4 Hill Street, EDINBURGH EH2 3JZ
Australia	Butterworths, SYDNEY, MELBOURNE, BRISBANE, ADELAIDE, PERTH, CANBERRA and HOBART
Canada	Butterworth Canada Ltd, TORONTO and VANCOUVER
Ireland	Butterworth (Ireland) Ltd, DUBLIN
Malaysia	Malayan Law Journal Sdn Bhd, KUALA LUMPUR
New Zealand	Butterworths of New Zealand Ltd, WELLINGTON and AUCKLAND
Puerto Rico	Butterworth of Puerto Rico, Inc, SAN JUAN
Singapore	Butterworths Asia, SINGAPORE
South Africa	Butterworths Publishers (Pty) Ltd, DURBAN
USA	Butterworth Legal Publishers, CARLSBAD, California; SALEM, New Hampshire

All rights reserved. No part of this publication may be reproduced in any material form (including photocopying or storing it in any medium by electronic means and whether or not transiently or incidentally to some other use of this publication) without the written permission of the copyright owner except in accordance with the provisions of the Copyright, Designs and Patents Act 1988 or under the terms of a licence issued by the Copyright Licensing Agency Ltd, 90 Tottenham Court Road, London, England, W1P 9HE. Application for the copyright owner's written permission to reproduce any part of this publication should be addressed to the publisher.

Warning: The doing of an unauthorised act in relation to a copyright work may result in both a civil claim for damages and criminal prosecution.

© Butterworth & Co (Publishers) Ltd 1994

A CIP catalogue record for this book is available from the British Library.

ISBN 0 406 04470 8

Printed and bound in Great Britain by Mackays of Chatham plc, Kent.

∞ This text paper meets the requirements of ISO 9706/1994. Information and Documentation—paper for documents—requirements for permanence.

Preface

The Sunday Trading Act 1994 received the Royal Assent on 5 July 1994. The Act, when implemented, will bring about fundamental changes in the law on Sunday trading but many of the concepts gathered from the Shops Act 1950 will remain of importance in the understanding of the new Act.

However, the 1994 Act is of importance not only because it sweeps away many restrictions on Sunday trading but also because new and substantial protection has been given to those working in shops on Sundays. The enforceability of those rights will no doubt be an issue before Industrial Tribunals in the not too distant future.

In this book I have tried therefore to give a clear and concise commentary on the Act, whilst comparing it with the provisions of the 1950 Act and, where appropriate, I have emphasised existing case law to demonstrate how it helps in the interpretation of the 1994 Act.

The way in which restrictions on Sunday trading developed, the efforts to amend the same, the parliamentary process and the very substantial legal challenges to the 1950 Act are all very important to having a good understanding of the 1994 Act. Where appropriate therefore, they have also been considered and explained. Whether this new legislation will produce a popular permanent and practical solution to the resolution of the issue of Sunday trading (as claimed by the supporters of the Act) will no doubt become apparent over the next few years. I hope that this book goes some way to introduce local authorities, retailers and lawyers to the concepts that will govern Sunday trading in the future.

I wish to give special thanks to all of my friends in retailing and especially Nigel Whittaker, Tim Clement-Jones, and David Ramsden of Kingfisher and everyone both past and present at B&Q plc. Without their support over the years my knowledge of this subject would have been much less and certainly not sufficient to consider writing this book.

To my friends at The Bar, especially David Vaughan QC, John Samuels QC, Gerald Barling QC, Nick Davidson QC, David Anderson and Malcolm Gibney, whose ideas appear often in this book, I express my gratitude for their generosity to me and their help in the 'battle'.

Finally, I give special acknowledgement to all at Hepherd, Winstanley & Pugh and especially those in the Sunday Trading Team—Kay Donalson, Christina Tovlas-Vincent, and Sara Davies, all of whom have contributed to this book and its presentation. Not least I must give a word of praise and thanks to my secretary, Stephanie LeBrun, whose management of this project has been excellent.

Tony Askham
1994

Contents

	Page
Preface	v
Table of Statutes	ix
Table of Cases	xiii
1 The history of the Shops Act 1950	1
2 What is a shop?	7
3 Small shops	20
4 Large shops	23
5 Exempt shops	29
6 The loading and unloading of lorries at large shops	37
7 Property law considerations	42
8 The Jewish exemption	45
9 The duties and powers of local authorities	48
10 The offences and defences	56
11 Shop worker protection	70
12 Existing Sunday work protection	84
13 Repeals	90
Appendix 1	
Sunday Trading Act 1994	95
Appendix 2	
Precedents	115
Index	121

Table of Statutes

References in this Table to *Statutes* are to Halsbury's Statutes of England (Fourth Edition) showing the volume and page at which the annotated text of an Act may be found.

	PARA
Business Names Act 1985 (48 *Statutes* 165)	
s 1	10.29
4(1)(b)	10.29
Cinemas Act 1985 (45 *Statutes* 734)	
s 9	12.5
Companies Act 1985 (8 *Statutes* 104)	
s 348	10.29
Consumer Protection Act 1987 (39 *Statutes* 188)	
s 24	10.64
27(1)	9.9
County Courts Act 1984 (11 *Statutes* 603)	
s 22	10.54
Employment Protection (Consolidation) Act 1978 (16 *Statutes* 232)	11.30
Pt II (ss 12–32)	11.77
s 22B	11.64
22C	11.65
Pt IV (ss 49–53)	11.75
Pt V (ss 54–80)	11.44
s 54	11.50
60A	11.67, 11.68
64(1)	11.50
129	11.77
141(2)	11.77
142	11.46
150	11.77
Sch 12	11.77
Sch 13	
para 9, 10, 20	11.35
Fire Precautions Act 1971 (35 *Statutes* 280)	
s 18(1)	9.9
Greater London Council (General Powers) Act 1981 (26 *Statutes* 820)	13.3
Greater London Council (General Powers) Act 1983 (26 *Statutes* 824)	13.3
Highways Act 1980 (20 *Statutes* 124)	6.4
s 329	5.19
Interpretation Act 1978 (41 *Statutes* 899)	
s 18	10.25

	PARA
Leasehold Property (Temporary Provisions) Act 1951	
s 10	2.14
20(1)	2.36
Licensing Act 1964 (24 *Statutes* 303)	
s 201(1)	5.6
Local Government Act 1972 (25 *Statutes* 168)	
s 222	9.27, 9.34, 9.35, 9.36, 9.37; 10.46, 10.47, 10.49, 10.51
Local Government (Miscellaneous Provisions) Act 1976 (38 *Statutes* 345)	
s 75(1)(c)	2.34
Local Government (Miscellaneous Provisions) Act 1982 (45 *Statutes* 680)	
Sch 3	
para 1(a)	6.15
Magistrates' Courts Act 1980 (27 *Statutes* 143)	
s 44	10.24
101	10.6
Marriage Act 1949 (37 *Statutes* 706)	
Pt IV (ss 53–67)	8.8
Medicines Act 1968 (28 *Statutes* 344)	5.13
s 74, 75, 130	5.12
Noise and Statutory Nuisance Act 1993	
Sch 2	
para 5	6.15
Pharmacy and Poisons Act 1933	12.5
Post Office Act 1969 (34 *Statutes* 439)	
Sch 4	13.8
Prevention of Oil Pollution Act 1971 (49 *Statutes* 170)	
s 19(1)(a)	9.9
Private Places of Entertainment (Licensing) Act 1967 (45 *Statutes* 641)	
s 7(2)	2.56
Protection from Eviction Act 1977 (23 *Statutes* 302)	
s 6	9.9

Table of statutes

	PARA
Public Order Act 1936 (12 *Statutes* 208)	9.9
Race Relations Act 1976 (6 *Statutes* 828)	
s 71(2)	9.9
Rating and Valuation (Apportionment) Act 1928	2.14
Sex Discrimination Act 1975 (6 *Statutes* 753)	1.14; 10.74, 10.77
Shop Hours Act 1892	2.5
s 9	2.6
Shop Hours Act 1904	2.5
Shops Act 1911	1.3
s 14	2.6
Shops Act 1936	2.11; 8.1; 9.18; 12.3
Shops Act 1950 (19 *Statutes* 388)	1.4, 1.9, 1.11; 2.1, 2.19, 2.23; 3.2; 5.1; 9.1, 9.4; 10.38
Pt I (ss 1–16)	3.19, 3.20, 3.21, 3.22; 5.17
s 1(7)	10.63
2	3.21; 4.12
(3)	10.63
18	2.35; 13.10
19	12.21, 12.22
22	12.3, 12.4, 12.5, 12.6, 12.7, 12.8, 12.11, 12.12, 12.13, 12.14, 12.20, 12.23; 13.10
(3)	12.15
Pt IV (ss 47–67)	1.20; 5.17; 7.6; 11.75, 11.82
s 47–66	12.15
47	3.21; 4.4, 4.5, 4.6; 9.22, 9.32; 10.5, 10.37, 10.47
50	10.5
53	8.1, 8.2, 8.4, 8.10
(2)	8.10
56(1)(a)	5.22
(3)	10.63
58	2.24; 5.31; 8.4
65	5.22
71	9.10, 9.20, 9.22, 9.27
(1)	10.48
(2)	9.30, 9.39; 10.39
(5)	10.19, 10.21, 10.22, 10.23, 10.24, 10.25
(6)	10.19, 10.23, 10.64, 10.65
(7)(b)	13.8
74	12.23
(1)	2.3; 12.8
Sch 3	
Pt I	12.22
Sch 5	1.2, 1.7; 4.11; 5.26, 5.28, 5.31; 7.6; 10.65; 13.2
Shops (Airports) Act 1962 (19 *Statutes* 569)	
s 1(1)	13.8

	PARA
Shops (Airports) Act 1962 – *contd*	
s 1(2)	5.17
Shops (Sunday Trading Restrictions) Act 1936	1.3; 2.11
Sunday Observance Act 1677	1.1, 1.2
Sunday Trading Act 1994	4.1; 9.38; 10.38
s 1	1.36
(1)	4.22
(2)	13.2
2	6.2, 6.5, 6.21, 6.23; 9.42
(3)	6.6
(4)	6.8
3	7.1, 7.3, 7.4, 7.5, 7.9, 7.10
(1), (2)	7.6
4	11.5
5	3.2, 3.3, 3.19
(1)	3.22
6	13.3
8	9.2
(2)	9.3
Sch 1	1.24; 2.61
para 1	2.29, 2.45; 3.2, 3.5; 4.19, 4.20; 5.4, 5.6, 5.33, 5.38
2(1)	4.2; 5.37, 5.38; 8.5, 8.12; 10.3, 10.5
(2)	4.2, 4.17
(a)	5.2
(b)	8.1, 8.5
(3)	4.2, 4.17, 4.26, 4.34; 10.3
(4)	4.18
3	5.2; 10.3
(1)	5.4
(a)	5.30
(b)	5.5, 5.6, 5.9
(c)	5.25
(d)	5.12
(e)	5.14
(f)	5.18
(g)	5.19
(h)	5.19, 5.21
(j)	5.22
(k)	5.33
(2)	5.35
(3)	5.14, 5.15
(4)	5.16, 5.17
(6)	5.17
4	4.17; 5.40; 6.11, 6.30; 9.6; 10.17
(1)	4.22, 4.25
(a)	4.28
(b)	4.27
(2)	4.29

Table of statutes

	PARA
Sunday Trading Act 1994 – *contd*	
Sch 1 – *contd*	
para 4(3)	4.23
5(1), (2)	9.5
(3)	9.5
(b)	9.6
6	4.32; 10.7
7(1)	8.12; 10.3, 10.4, 10.5, 10.35
(2)	10.7, 10.35
8	10.63
9	4.23
Sch 2	
para 1	9.8
2	9.30, 9.39
3	9.44
4	9.47; 10.9, 10.10
5	10.33, 10.73
6	10.26
(1)	10.18, 10.21, 10.22, 10.23
(2)	9.42; 10.19
7	10.64
(1)	10.64
(2)	10.73
Pt II (paras 8–10)	8.1, 8.13; 9.40, 9.48
para 8(1), (4)	8.14
(5), (6)	9.41
(7)	8.11
(10)	9.48; 10.11, 10.12
(11)	8.17; 9.48
(12)	8.8
9	8.5, 8.9
10(1), (2)	8.10
Sch 3	6.2, 6.5, 6.8, 6.15, 6.29; 9.42, 9.49
para 2	6.32; 10.16
3(1)	6.19
(2)	6.24
4	6.13
6(1)	6.17
(2)	6.20
7(a), (b)	6.24
8	6.21
9	6.26; 10.15
Sch 4	2.26; 5.1; 11.5, 11.25, 11.72, 11.77, 11.87; 12.11
para 1	11.5
(1)	11.6, 11.7, 11.13, 11.14, 11.16, 11.17, 11.23, 11.38
(2)	11.20
(a)	11.21
(b)	11.22
(3)	11.22

	PARA
Sunday Trading Act 1994 – *contd*	
Sch 4 – *contd*	
para 2	11.25
(2)	11.26, 11.29
(a), (b)	11.34
(3)	11.27, 11.29
(4)	11.30
(6)	11.33
3	11.37
(1)(b)	11.38
(2)	11.38
4	11.40
5(1)	11.42
(c)	11.42
(2)	11.42
(5)	11.43
6	11.41
7	11.44
(1)	11.44
(2), (3)	11.45
9	11.50
10	11.51, 11.63, 11.64, 11.77
(5)	11.53
(6)	11.61
11	11.78
(4)	11.81
12	11.82
(3), (4)	11.83
13	11.82, 11.84
14	11.53, 11.54, 11.55, 11.82, 11.86
15	11.53, 11.57, 11.60, 11.82, 11.86
16	11.63
17	11.73
18	11.75
19	11.67
20	11.74
21	11.76
22	11.77
23	12.5, 12.15
24	13.4
Sch 5	13.8
Trade Descriptions Act 1968 (39 *Statutes* 41)	
s 20(1)	10.22
26(1)	9.9
39(1)	2.56
Trade Union Reform and Employment Rights Act 1993	11.63, 11.69
Transport Act 1968 (38 *Statutes* 185)	
s 10(1)(xvii)	2.34
Tyne and Wear Act 1976	13.3
Wages Act 1986 (16 *Statutes* 523)	11.90

Table of statutes

	PARA
Weights and Measures Act 1985 (50 *Statutes* 9)	
s 83	10.38

	PARA
West Midlands County Council Act 1980	13.3

Table of Cases

A

Associated Provincial Picture Houses Ltd v Wednesbury Corpn [1948] 1 KB 223, [1947] 2 All ER 680, [1948] LJR 190, 177 LT 641, 112 JP 55, 63 TLR 623, 92 Sol Jo 26, 45 LGR 635, CA 8.17

Avon County Council v Buscott [1988] QB 656, [1988] 1 All ER 841, [1988] 2 WLR 788, 132 Sol Jo 567, 86 LGR 569, 20 HLR 385, [1988] 14 LS Gaz R 49, CA 9.36

B

B & Q (Retail) Ltd v Dudley Metropolitan Borough Council (1987) 86 LGR 137, [1988] BTLC 420 .... 10.6

Baxters (Butchers) Ltd v Manley (1985) 4 Tr L 219 .... 10.71

Berthelemy v Neale [1952] 1 All ER 437, [1952] 1 TLR 458, 96 Sol Jo 165, CA 2.37

Betta Cars Ltd v Ilford Corpn (1959) 124 JP 19, 103 Sol Jo 834 .... 4.5, 4.9

Bibby-Cheshire v Golden Wonder Ltd [1972] 3 All ER 738, [1972] 1 WLR 1487, 137 JP 15, 116 Sol Jo 842, 70 LGR 601 .... 10.71

Binns v Wardale [1946] KB 451, 115 LJKB 427, 175 LT 178, 110 JP 246, 90 Sol Jo 332, sub nom Wardale v Binns [1946] 2 All ER 100, 62 TLR 424, 44 LGR 241 .... 1.7

Blackpool Borough Council v W H Smith Do-It-All Ltd (28 July 1987, unreported) 1.7

Boyd v A Bell & Sons Ltd 1970 JC 1, 1969 SLT 156 .... 2.16

Bromley v Tryon [1952] AC 265, [1951] 2 All ER 1058, [1951] 2 TLR 1119, HL 2.38

C

Chichester District Council v Flockglen Ltd (1977) 122 Sol Jo 61 .... 8.4

Chisholm v Kirklees Metropolitan Borough Council [1993] ICR 826 .... 1.14, 10.77

Colchester Borough Council v W H Smith Do-It-All Ltd (28 July 1987, unreported) 1.7

Collman v Roberts [1896] 1 QB 457, 65 LJMC 63, 74 LT 198, 60 JP 184, 44 WR 445, 12 TLR 202, 18 Cox CC 273 .... 2.4

Cowlairs Co-operative Society v Glasgow Corpn 1957 JC 51, 1957 SLT 288 .... 2.24

Criminal proceedings against Tankstation't Heukske VOF and JBE Boermans, Re: C–401, 402/92 unreported 1.13

D

Deeble v Robinson [1954] 1 QB 77, [1953] 2 All ER 1348, [1953] 3 WLR 975, 97 Sol Jo 812, CA 2.37

Dennis v Hutchinson [1922] 1 KB 693, [1922] All ER 455, 91 LJKB 584, 86 JP 85, 126 LT 669, 38 TLR 263, 66 Sol Jo 316, 20 LGR 199, 27 Cox CC 202 .... 2.24

Table of Cases

Dieci v Sindaco del Comune di Madignano: C–24/94 unreported 1.13

E

Eldorado Ice Cream Co Ltd v Clark [1938] 1 KB 715, [1938] 1 All ER 330, 107 LJKB 290, 158 LT 249, 102 JP 147, 54 TLR 356, 82 Sol Jo 176, 36 LGR 203, 30 Cox CC 660 . . . . 2.24
Erewash Borough Council v Ilkeston Co-operative Society Ltd (1988) 153 JP 141, 87 LGR 96, [1989] Crim LR 157 . . . . 2.4, 2.18
Evans v Texas Homecare Ltd (1987) 152 JP 268, 86 LGR 577, [1988] BTLC 426 . . 1.7
Evans & Co Ltd v LCC [1914] 3 KB 315, 83 LJKB 1264, 111 LT 288, 78 JP 345, 30 TLR 509, 24 Cox CC 290, 12 LGR 1079 . . . . 10.28

F

Fawcett Properties Ltd v Buckingham County Council [1961] AC 636, [1960] 3 All ER 503, [1960] 3 WLR 831, 125 JP 8, 104 Sol Jo 912, 59 LGR 69, 12 P & CR 1, 176 Estates Gazette 1115, HL 2.38
Fine-Fare Ltd v Brighton County Borough Council [1959] 1 All ER 476, [1959] 1 WLR 223, 123 JP 197, 103 Sol Jo 179 . . . . 2.65
Frawley (M & F) Ltd v Ve-Ri-Best Manufacturing Co Ltd [1953] 1 QB 318, [1953] 1 All ER 50, [1953] 1 WLR 165, 97 Sol Jo 46, 3 P & CR 301, CA 2.14

G

George v James [1914] 1 KB 278, 83 LJKB 303, 110 LT 316, 78 JP 156, 30 TLR 230, 12 LGR 403, 24 Cox CC 48 . . . . 12.9
George v PBI (International) Ltd (3 October 1991, unreported) 12.2
Gouriet v Union of Post Office Workers [1978] AC 435, [1977] 3 All ER 70, [1977] 3 WLR 300, 141 JP 552, 121 Sol Jo 543, HL. 10.38, 10.43, 10.44
Greenwood v Whelan [1967] 1 QB 396, [1967] 1 All ER 294, [1967] 2 WLR 289, 111 Sol Jo 52, 65 LGR 58 . . . . 2.24

H

Hadley v Texas Homecare Ltd (1987) 152 JP 268, 86 LGR 577, [1988] BTLC 426, [1988] Crim LR 318 . . . . 1.7
Harris v Amery (1865) LR 1 CP 148, Hop & Ph 294, Har & Ruth 357, 35 LJCP 89, 13 LT 504, 30 JP 56, 12 Jur NS 165, 14 WR 199 . . . . 2.4
Havering London Borough Council v L F Stone & Son Ltd (1973) 117 Sol Jo 893, 72 LGR 223, [1973] Crim LR 770 . . . . 4.12
Hesketh v Wallasey Corpn [1954] 2 All ER 187, [1954] 1 WLR 771, 118 JP 287, 98 Sol Jo 338, 52 LGR 326 . . . . 4.5
Hoffmann-La Roche & Co AG v Secretary of State for Trade and Industry [1975] AC 295, [1974] 2 All ER 1128, [1974] 3 WLR 104, 118 Sol Jo 500, HL 10.56
Hudson v Marshall (1977) 75 LGR 13 . . . . 1.7

I

Ilford Corpn v Betterclean (Seven Kings) Ltd [1965] 2 QB 222, [1965] 1 All ER 900, [1965] 2 WLR 727, 129 JP 271, 109 Sol Jo 253, 63 LGR 208 . . . . 2.15, 4.4
Imperial Tobacco Ltd v A-G [1981] AC 718, [1980] 1 All ER 866, [1980] 2 WLR 466, 124 Sol Jo 271, HL 10.45

J

Jarmain v Wetherell (1977) 121 Sol Jo 153, 75 LGR 537 . . . .   2.24

K

Keck and Mithoud, Re: C-262, 268/91 unreported, ECJ 10.76
Kirklees Metropolitan Borough Council v B & Q plc [1993] ICR 826 . . . . .   1.14, 10.77
Kirklees Metropolitan Borough Council v Wickes Building Supplies Ltd [1990] 1 WLR 1237, [1990] 2 CMLR 501, 134 Sol Jo 1152, 88 LGR 968; on appeal sub nom Kirklees Borough Council v Wickes Building Supplies Ltd [1993] AC 227, [1991] 4 All ER 240, [1991] 3 WLR 985, [1991] 3 CMLR 282, 89 LGR 872, CA; revsd sub nom Kirklees Metropolitan Borough Council v Wickes Building Supplies Ltd [1993] AC 227, [1992] 3 All ER 717, [1992] 3 WLR 170, [1992] 2 CMLR 765, 90 LGR 391, [1992] NLJR 967, HL. 9.27, 10.48, 10.58, 10.59, 10.60

L

Lewis and Lewis v Roger (1984) 148 JP 481, 82 LGR 670 . . . .   2.12, 2.17
Liverpool Corpn v Peter Walker & Son Ltd (1913) 77 JP Jo 402 . . . .   10.28
LCC v Davis [1938] 2 All ER 764, 159 LT 44, 102 JP 347, 54 TLR 845, 82 Sol Jo 567, 36 LGR 564, 31 Cox CC 77 . . . .   1.6, 1.7
LCC v Iafrate [1939] 1 All ER 191, 160 LT 281, 103 JP 89, 55 TLR 369, 83 Sol Jo 177, 37 LGR 187. . . . .   1.7
LCC v Lees [1939] 1 All ER 191, 160 LT 281, 103 JP 89, 55 TLR 369, 83 Sol Jo 177, 37 LGR 187. . . . .   1.6, 1.7
LCC v Wettman [1922] 1 KB 153, 91 LJKB 77, 126 LT 336, 86 JP 4, 38 TLR 67, 66 Sol Jo 19, 19 LGR 781, 27 Cox CC 148. . . . .   12.9
Luton Borough Council v Texas Homecare Ltd (1987) 152 JP 268, 86 LGR 577, [1988] BTLC 426. . . . .   1.7

M

Maby v Warwick Corpn [1972] 2 QB 242, [1972] 2 All ER 1198, [1972] 3 WLR 25, 116 Sol Jo 445, 71 LGR 436, [1972] Crim LR 450 . . . .   2.24
Madeley (Paul) Ltd v Leeds City Council (1987) 152 JP 268, 86 LGR 577, [1988] BTLC 426. . . . .   1.7
Modaffari v Comune di Cinisello Balsamo: C–14/94 unreported 1.13
Modaffari v Sindaco del Comune di Osio Sopra: C–23/94 unreported 1.13
Monaco Garage Ltd v Watford Borough Council [1967] 2 All ER 1291, [1967] 1 WLR 1069, 131 JP 446, 111 Sol Jo 471, 65 LGR 424 . . . .   4.5
Moore v Tweedale [1935] 2 KB 163, 104 LJKB 594, 153 LT 96, 99 JP 221, 51 TLR 437, 79 Sol Jo 288, 33 LGR 216, 30 Cox CC 229. . . . .   10.63
Morton v Wickes Building Supplies Ltd (1987) 152 JP 268, 86 LGR 577, [1988] BTLC 426 . . . .   1.7

N

Newberry v Cohen's (Smoked Salmon) Ltd (1956) 54 LGR 343 . . . .   1.7
Newport Borough Council v Khan [1990] 1 WLR 1185, [1991] 1 EGLR 287, CA. 10.54
North West Leicestershire District Council v Gramlo Ltd (13 May 1988, unreported), CA 1.8, 2.19, 8.4

Table of Cases

O

Oberst v Coombs (1955) 53 LGR 316 . . . . 10.38

P

Pope v Whalley (1865) 6 B & S 303, 5 New Rep 323, 34 LJMC 76, 11 LT 769, 29
  JP 134, 11 Jur NS 444, 13 WR 402 . . . . 2.4
Punto Casa SpA v Sindaco del Comune di Capena and Comune di Capena: C–69,
  258/93 unreported 1.13

Q

Quattordici v Commissario Straodinario del Comune di Terlizzi: C–9/94 unreported: 1.13

R

R v Braintree District Council, ex p Willingham (1982) 81 LGR 70 . . . . 9.20
R v Harrow Justices, ex p Woolworths plc (14 July 1994, unreported) 10.37
R v Norwich Justices, ex p Texas Homecare [1991] Crim LR 555, [1991] COD 318: 10.40
R v South Somerset District Council, ex p DJB (Group) Ltd (1989) 87 LGR 624 . . 9.31
R v Thurrock Borough Council, ex p Tesco Stores plc (1993) 137 Sol Jo LB 276 . . 2.22
Randall v D Turner (Garages) Ltd [1973] 3 All ER 369, [1973] 1 WLR 1052, 117 Sol
  Jo 446, 71 LGR 465, [1973] Crim LR 535. . . . . 2.24
Reading Borough Council v Payless DIY Ltd: C–304/90 [1992] ECR I–6493, [1993]
  1 CMLR 426, ECJ 1.12
Ritz Cleaners Ltd v West Middlesex Assessment Committee [1937] 2 KB 642, [1937]
  2 All ER 368, 106 LJKB 398, 157 LT 423, 101 JP 307, 53 TLR 588, 81 Sol Jo
  337, 35 LGR 309, CA 2.14
Rochdale Borough Council v Anders: C–306/88 [1993] 1 All ER 520n, [1993]
  1 CMLR 426, ECJ 1.12
Rochford District Council v Texas Homecare Ltd (1987) 152 JP 268, 86 LGR 577,
  [1988] BTLC 426 . . . . 1.7

S

Salford Cattle Market Salerooms Ltd v Osborne (1923) 92 LJKB 1018, [1923] All ER
  Rep 312, 129 LT 686, 87 JP 134, 21 LGR 468, 27 Cox CC 515 . . . . 10.63
Salisbury District Council v RMC Homecare (South) Ltd (1987) 152 JP 268, 86 LGR
  577, [1988] BTLC 426 . . . . 1.7
Semeraro Casa Uno v Sindaco del Comune di Erbusco: C–418/93 unreported. . . . 1.13
Smith v Anderson (1880) 15 Ch D 247, [1874–0] All ER Rep 1121, 50 LJ Ch 39, 43
  LT 329, 29 WR 21, CA 2.4
Smith v Hayle Town Council [1978] ICR 996, [1978] IRLR 413, 122 Sol Jo 642, 77
  LGR 52, CA 11.71
South Tyneside Metropolitan Borough Council v Ritz Video Film Hire Ltd
  unreported. 2.19
Steadman v Hogg-Robinson Ltd (1993) unreported, EAT 12.1
Stoke-on-Trent City Council v B & Q (Retail) Ltd [1984] Ch 1, [1984] 2 All ER 787,
  [1983] 3 WLR 78, 127 Sol Jo 426, 82 LGR 10, CA; affd [1984] AC 754, [1984]
  2 All ER 332, [1984] 2 WLR 929, 128 Sol Jo 364, 82 LGR 473, 4 Tr L 9,
  HL. 9.21, 9.24, 9.34, 10.44, 10.47, 10.50

Table of Cases

Stoke-on-Trent City Council v B & Q plc: C–169/91 [1993] AC 900, [1993] 1 All ER 481, [1993] 2 WLR 730, [1992] ECR I–6635, [1993] 1 CMLR 426, 91 LGR 237, ECJ; affd sub nom Stoke-on-Trent City Council v B & Q plc [1993] AC 900, [1993] 2 All ER 297n, [1993] 2 WLR 730, [1993] 2 CMLR 509, 137 Sol Jo LB 120, 91 LGR 237, HL 1.12, 10.75
Stoke-on-Trent City Council v W H Smith Do-It-All Ltd (28 July 1987, unreported): 1.7
Stone v Boreham [1959] 1 QB 1, [1958] 2 All ER 715, [1958] 3 WLR 209, 122 JP 418, 102 Sol Jo 548 . . . . 2.24
Summers v Roberts [1944] KB 106, [1943] 2 All ER 757, 113 LJKB 109, 170 LT 130, 108 JP 52, 60 TLR 102, 88 Sol Jo 36, 42 LGR 54 . . . . 2.24

T

Tameside Metropolitan Borough Council v W H Smith Do-It-All Ltd (1987) 152 JP 268, 86 LGR 577, [1988] BTLC 426 . . . . 1.7
Tesco Stores plc v Kirklees Metropolitan Borough Council (27 July 1993, unreported) 9.32
Tesco Supermarkets Ltd v Nattrass [1972] AC 153, [1971] 2 All ER 127, [1971] 2 WLR 1166, 135 JP 289, 115 Sol Jo 285, 69 LGR 403, HL 10.21, 10.70
Thanet District Council v Ninedrive Ltd [1978] 1 All ER 703, 142 JP 188, 121 Sol Jo 706, 76 LGR 320 . . . . 8.4
Tonkin v Raven [1959] 1 QB 177, [1958] 3 All ER 374, [1958] 3 WLR 643, 123 JP 10, 102 Sol Jo 845, 56 LGR 447 . . . . 10.5
Torfaen Borough Council v B and Q plc: C–145/88 [1990] 2 QB 19, [1990] 1 All ER 129, [1990] 2 WLR 1330, [1989] ECR 3851, [1990] 1 CMLR 337, 134 Sol Jo 908, 88 LGR 649, [1990] 9 LS Gaz R 41, ECJ 1.11
Transworld Land Co Ltd v J Sainsbury plc [1990] 2 EGLR 255 . . . . 7.10
Treacher & Co Ltd v Treacher [1874] WN 4 . . . . 2.21

W

Ward v W H Smith & Son [1913] 3 KB 154, 82 LJKB 941, 109 LT 439, 77 JP 370, 29 TLR 536, 11 LGR 741, 23 Cox CC 562 . . . . 12.18
Waterman v Wallasey Corpn [1954] 2 All ER 187, [1954] 1 WLR 771, 118 JP 287, 98 Sol Jo 338, 52 LGR 326 . . . . 4.5
Waverley Borough Council v Hilden [1988] 1 All ER 807, [1988] 1 WLR 246, 132 Sol Jo 192, 86 LGR 271, [1988] JPL 175, [1988] 8 LS Gaz R 36 . . . . 9.36
Wickes Building Supplies Ltd v Kirklees Metropolitan District Council (1983) 148 JP 106, 82 LGR 467 . . . . 10.39

Y

Yeovil District Council v DJB (Martock) Ltd (5 March 1982, unreported) 4.6

Table of Cases

Decisions of the European Court of Justice are listed below numerically

These decisions are also included in the preceding alphabetical Table.

C–145/88: Torfaen Borough Council v B and Q plc [1990] 2 QB 19, [1990] 1 All ER 129, [1990] 2 WLR 1330, [1989] ECR 3851, [1990] 1 CMLR 337, 134 Sol Jo 908, 88 LGR 649, [1990] 9 LS Gaz R 41, ECJ	1.11
C–306/88: Rochdale Borough Council v Anders [1993] 1 All ER 520n, [1993] 1 CMLR 426, ECJ	1.12
C–304/90: Reading Borough Council v Payless DIY Ltd [1992] ECR I–6493, [1993] 1 CMLR 426, ECJ	1.12
C–169/91: Stoke-on-Trent City Council v B & Q plc [1993] AC 900, [1993] 1 All ER 481, [1993] 2 WLR 730, [1992] ECR I–6635, [1993] 1 CMLR 426, 91 LGR 237, ECJ; affd sub nom Stoke-on-Trent City Council v B & Q plc [1993] AC 900, [1993] 2 All ER 297n, [1993] 2 WLR 730, [1993] 2 CMLR 509, 137 Sol Jo LB 120, 91 LGR 237, HL	1.12
C–262, 268/91: Re Keck and Mithoud unreported, ECJ	10.76
C–401, 402/92: Re Criminal proceedings against Tankstation't Heukske VOF and JBE Boermans unreported	1.13
C–69, 258/93: Punto Casa SpA v Sindaco del Comune di Capena and Comune di Capena unreported	1.13
C–418/93: Semeraro Casa Uno v Sindaco del Comune di Erbusco unreported.	1.13
C–9/94: Quattordici v Commissario Straodinario del Comune di Terlizzi unreported:	1.13
C–14/94: Modaffari v Comune di Cinisello Balsamo unreported	1.13
C–23/94: Modaffari v Sindaco del Comune di Osio Sopra unreported	1.13
C–24/94: Dieci v Sindaco del Comune di Madignano unreported	1.13

The history of the Shops Act 1950

INTRODUCTION

1.1 It has been said with considerable truth that it took some 60 years for Parliament to enact legislation to restrict retail trading on Sundays and a further 60 years to undo the harm that it had caused. The restrictions on Sunday trading had their principal expression in the Sunday Observance Act 1677 which was not repealed until 1969. However, in the latter part of the 19th century many efforts were made by MPs to bring forward legislation to restrict Sunday trading and in particular to protect shopworkers from working excessive hours. Work done at the beginning of this century showed that many shopworkers, many of whom lived above the shop, were working in excess of 80 hours a week. Although it had improved, the position was still unsatisfactory in 1930.[1]

[1] Report from Select Committee on Shop Assistants (HMSO 30.7.1930; 18.9.1931).

1.2 This led to a number of Acts of Parliament dealing with shop hours and to the setting up of a Select Committee of the House of Commons with a Committee of the House of Lords to inquire into the subject of Sunday trading. These Committees presented a report in July 1906.[1] From this report it was clear that Sunday trading was widespread at the end of the 19th century. Chief constables who gave evidence made it clear that few of them were trying to enforce the Sunday Observance Act but in Hull the police had made a consistent and persistent attempt to enforce the law, having carried out 4,235 prosecutions of over 200 shops in 1904 alone. The Committee set out in its report some proposed exemptions which appear to be the historical beginnings of the much maligned Fifth Schedule to the Shops Act 1950.

[1] Report of the Select Committee appointed to join with a Committee of the House of Lords to inquire into the subject of Sunday Trading (19.7.1906).

1.3 In 1905[1] and 1911[2] the Government attempted to bring forward restrictions on Sunday trading but on both occasions without success. Finally, a Private Member's Bill, enacted as the Shops (Sunday Trading Restrictions) Act 1936, brought into effect the restrictions on Sunday trading which have lasted until the enactment of the Sunday Trading Act 1994.

[1] The Sunday Closing (Shops) Bill 1905.
[2] The Shops Act 1911 contained provisions restricting Sunday trading until Standing Committee stage when the clauses were 'left out'.

1.4 The Shops Act 1950 merely consolidated various Acts on shop closing hours (including the 1936 Act) and did not make any alterations to the Schedule of exemptions or to the detailed provisions of the 1936 legislation. The Act was the product of a joint Select Committee of both Houses.[1] Its passage through Parliament was uneventful.

1.4 The history of the Shops Act 1950

[1] The Commons Committee 'Closing Hours of Shops' (Cmd 7105, April 1947).

1.5 It appears always to have been the position of the MPs responsible for the 1936 Act that there had to be considerable exemptions. Most members seemed to accept there was a need to purchase food on Sundays and also that certain other convenient and expected products such as tobacco should also be available.

1.6 Attempts to produce a workable list of exemptions have failed to stand the test of time. Indeed within a few years of the passing of the 1936 Act it became the subject of trenchant judicial criticism. As an example, in 1936 Humphries J in *LCC v Davis*[1] summarised the problem as follows—

> 'There is almost no nonsensical proposition which might not be seriously put forward as a result of looking at these innumerable exceptions.'

[1] [1938] 2 All ER 764 at 766. See also *LCC v Lees* [1939] 1 All ER 191 at 194, per Hewart LCJ.

1.7 As a result, there has been much litigation over the years as to the type of goods which could lawfully be sold on Sundays and the courts have had to make very difficult decisions on issues such as whether certain items in a DIY store were or were not motor accessories within the exemption in the Fifth Schedule[1] or which products fell within the expression 'meal or refreshment'[2] and what were 'souvenirs'[3] within the additional list of goods which could be sold in holiday resorts.

[1] *Blackpool Borough Council v WH Smith Do-It-All Ltd; Colchester BC v WH Smith Do-It-All Ltd; Stoke o Trent City Council of v WH Smith Do-It-All Ltd*, judgment unreported. See also, *Hadley v Texas Homecare Ltd; Evans v Texas Homecare Ltd; Salisbury District Council v RMC Homecare (South) Ltd; Morton v Wicke Building Supplies Ltd; Rochford District Council v Texas Homecare Ltd; Luton Borough Council v Texa Homecare Ltd; Paul Madeley Ltd v Leeds City Council; Tameside Metropolitan Borough Council v WH Smith Do-It-All Ltd* (1987) 152 JP 268, 86 LGR 577.

[2] *LCC v Davis* [1938] 2 All ER 764 (newly cooked rolls and bread came within 'newly cooked provisions'). *LCC v Lees* and *LCC v Iafrate* [1939] 1 All ER 191 (fruitcake, swiss roll, veal and ham pies, currant buns and pastries all capable of being meals or refreshments). *Binns v Wardale* [1946] KB 451, sub nom *Wardale v Binns* [1946] 2 All ER 100 (a loaf of bread is a meal or refreshment). *Newberry v Cohen's (Smoked Salmon) Ltd* (1956) 54 LGR 343 (a partly cooked kipper was a meal or refreshment but a packet of tea or flour was not).

[3] *Hudson v Marshall* (1977) 75 LGR 13 (tee shirt emblazoned with a 'Bugs Bunny' motif was within the exception).

1.8 In addition, other provisions of the Act were extremely complex. Judicial criticism in this respect is highlighted by an unreported judgment of the Court of Appeal[1] in which Lord Justice Mann stated—

> 'It is not for this Court to pronounce upon the merits of trading on a Sunday but the Court does observe the present situation brings the law into disrepute. This is first because the Act of 1950 is being strained to cover places which it may be doubted were within the legislative intent. Second, because of differential enforcement and third because of the curious miscellany of exempt transactions which no member of the public can readily understand.'

[1] *North West Leicestershire District Council v Gramlo Ltd & Another* (13 May 1988, unreported) judgment of the Court of Appeal.

1.9 It is apparent that the 1950 Act was introduced following the Gowers Committee Report,[1] when it was decided to consolidate the legislation whilst the complexities of the problem were considered. Following more detailed recommendations of this Committee, the Government attempted to reform the law in 1956 but failed in the Commons because of a lack of Parliamentary time. A further Departmental Committee appointed in 1961[2] under the Chairmanship of Lord Crathorne resulted in the publication of a discussion paper entitled 'Retail Trading Hours'. Because of opposition from the Union of Shops Distributive and Allied Workers (USDAW) and part of the retail trade it was abandoned. Between then and the 1985 Shops Bill, there were 18 attempts to amend the Shops Act, all of which failed.

[1] Cmd 7105 (April 1947).
[2] The 'Report of the Departmental Committee on the Law on Sunday Observance' (Cmnd 2528, December 1964).

1.10 In 1982 the Government set up the Auld Committee which published a report in November 1984.[1] The Auld Committee Report recommended the total abolition of restrictions on Sunday trading and the House of Commons, by an overwhelming majority of 304 to 184, accepted the case for the reform of the legislation on shopping hours and looked forward to the Government bringing forward legislation to remove such restrictions.[2] As a result of that indication, the Government brought forward the 1985 Shops Bill. The Bill was presented first in the House of Lords and passed through with minor amendments. In an historic Second Reading[3] in the House of Commons it was lost by a vote of 282 to 296.

[1] Report of the Committee of Inquiry into proposals to amend the Shops Acts. Chairman Mr Robin Auld QC Cmnd 9376 November 1984.
[2] HC Deb, 20 May 1985, col 745.
[3] HC 2R, 14 April 1986, col 558.

1.11 Not only were there attempts in Parliament to change the law and much litigation in the English courts on the provisions of the Act itself, but between 1988 and 1992 there was substantial litigation on the issue of whether or not the restrictions on Sunday trading infringed Article 30 of the EC Treaty. In all, between 1988 and 1989 12 courts (in England and Wales and Northern Ireland) including the High Court referred the issue to the European Court of Justice who in its judgment in the case of *Torfaen Borough Council v B & Q plc*[1] accepted that the Sunday trading ban contained in the Shops Act 1950 fell within the scope of Article 30 and indicated that it was a matter of fact for the national court to decide whether the ban was both justified and proportionate.

[1] *Torfaen Borough Council v B & Q plc* Case C-145/88 [1990] 2 QB 19, [1990] 1 All ER 129.

1.12 Further litigation proceeded as a result of this judgment until the matter was referred back to the European Court by the House of Lords in the matter of *Stoke-on-Trent City Council and Norwich City Council v B & Q plc*.[1] The European Court in that case finally decided itself, in an apparent volte-face, that the 1950 Act was both justified and proportionate.

[1] *Stoke-on-Trent City Council v B & Q plc* Case C-169/91 [1993] AC 900, 1 All ER 481. See also *Rochdale Borough Council v Anders* Case C-306/88, [1993] 1 All ER 520 n; *Reading Borough Council v Payless DIY Ltd* Case, C-304/90 [1992] ECR I-6493, [1993] 1 CMLR 426.

1.13 The history of the Shops Act 1950

1.13 Similar challenges to the Sunday trading laws in France, Belgium and Italy and to evening trading laws in Holland, have all been the subject of references to the ECJ, suggesting the respective national rules are contrary to Article 30 of the EC Treaty.[1] To date, all have failed.

---

[1] See for instance, Joined Cases C-69/93 and C-258/93 *Punto Casa SpA v Sindaco del Comune di Capena and Comune di Capena*; Case C-418/93 *Semeraro Casa Uno v Sindaco del Comune di Erbusco*; Case C-14/94 *Modaffari v Comune di Cinisello Balsamo*; Case C-9/94 *M Quattordici v Commissario Straodinario del Comune di Terlizzi*; Case C-23/94 *Modaffari v Sindaco del Comune di Osio Sopra*; Case C-24/94 *M Dieci v Sindaco del Comune di Madignano and Joined Cases C-401 and 402/92 Criminal Proceedings against one Tankstation't Heukske VOF and JBE Boermans* (Advocate General's Opinions in this Dutch case and in one of the Italian cases were given on the 16 March 1993, but the judgments of the Court in these two cases has not yet been given).

1.14 Following the judgment of the European Court further challenges were mounted stating that the effect of the 1950 Act was to discriminate against female shop workers and in particular female part time shop workers[1] and as a result was contrary to the Sex Discrimination Act 1975 and the EC Equal Treatment Directive and hence 'of no effect'.

---

[1] *Chisholm v Kirklees Metropolitan Borough Council; Kirklees Metropolitan Borough Council v B & Q plc*, [1993] ICR 826.

THE BACKGROUND TO THE NEW LAW

1.15 Following the defeat of the Bill in 1986, and the repeated challenges to the legality of the Act itself in the European Court and the English courts, the Government, upon re-election, pledged to try to bring sense to the law on Sunday trading.

1.16 The 1986 Bill had largely been defeated by a magnificent lobby campaign by a campaigning group called the Keep Sunday Special Campaign (KSSC). Following its success in this respect, a rival organisation, the Shopping Hours Reform Council (SHRC), was established to put forward the views of retailers who were in favour of some form of deregulation and of consumer organisations, who shared similar views. Late in 1992 a further organisation, Retailers for Shops Act Reform (RSAR), headed by Marks & Spencer plc, entered the ring with its own proposals.

1.17 Because the subject was one which was known to divide all political parties in Parliament, the Government from an early stage indicated that it intended to allow a free vote on the major clauses of the Bill which related to shopping hours themselves, whilst retaining the right to whip those which related to employment protection.

1.18 In July 1993 the Government published a consultation document on the possible options for reform. That document explained the four main options: total deregulation; the KSSC option; the RSAR option; and the SHRC option. It also set out possible draft legislation to put those options into effect.[1] In November 1993 the Sunday Trading Bill itself was published which by then included three options to reform, the proposals of RSAR having been amalgamated with those of the KSSC.

---

[1] 'Reforming the Law on Sunday Trading. A Guide to the Options for Reform' (Cmnd 2300, July 1993).

The background to the new law 1.28

1.19 It is not necessary in this book to describe in detail each of the three options, but because of the amendments to the Bill during its parliamentary progress it is perhaps useful for the reader to have some understanding of those options.

Option 1—Total deregulation

1.20 This option would have repealed the Shops Act 1950, Pt IV, and thus swept away all restrictions on Sunday opening for all shops whilst giving protection to shopworkers.

Option 2—The regulatory scheme

1.21 By the time the Bill had been published it involved an amalgamation of the proposals of the KSSC and of RSAR. These proposals were extremely complex but in essence they extended considerably the meaning of a 'shop' and prevented all large shops from opening on Sundays other than for the four Sundays before Christmas.

1.22 Certain shops irrespective of size were exempt. Small shops, ie those under 280 square metres and of a certain type, provided they sold certain goods (and in some cases were able to comply with further conditions), could also open.

1.23 The proposals also purported to allow garden centres, motor supply and motor accessory shops and DIY stores to open, although because of the complexities of their drafting it was difficult to know whether they would have achieved their objectives. There were substantial fines for infringement, in the sum of £50,000.

Option 3—SHRC proposals

1.24 These now form the basis of Sch 1 to the 1994 Act. They had been specifically designed for ease of enforcement. Certain shops were totally exempted through two mechanisms, first, by an amendment to the definition of a 'shop' in the 1950 Act, effectively excluding all service industries and retail sectors where the prime trade was the hire of goods; secondly, by specific exemptions for shops which must be able to open on Sundays throughout the day.

1.25 All small shops without exception were allowed to open and large shops could open for a continuous period of six hours between 10.00am and 6.00pm.

The Parliamentary procedure used

1.26 The procedure used by the Government to take the Bill through Parliament was unusual and may become a blueprint for Parliamentary procedure for highly contentious issues of conscience which are not to be dealt with strictly on party lines.

1.27 The Bill was initially given a Second Reading on the general principle of the requirement to reform the law. An overwhelming majority was obtained at the Second Reading for the Bill itself.

1.28 The matter then came before a Committee of the whole House of Commons to vote for the option. The voting started with a vote on total deregulation which was lost (174 for and 404 against). The next vote was on the KSSC/RSAR option which

1.28 *The history of the Shops Act 1950*

was again lost, this time by a majority of 18 (286 for and 304 against). On the SHRC Option, there was a majority in favour of 75 (333 for and 258 against).

1.29 Thereafter the Bill went into its usual Standing Committee stage from which it emerged with only one major amendment which was to increase the level of fines for non-compliance from £5,000 to £50,000.

1.30 The next stage was a further Committee of the whole House to deal with the Fourth Schedule to the Bill which gave worker protection. Following that, the matter then reverted to the Commons itself for the Report Stage and Third Reading.

1.31 The whole process was then repeated in the Lords with a Second Reading on 8 March 1994 and an Options Debate on 29 March 1994 in which the Lords chose the SHRC option. (On the total deregulation option the voting was 46 for and 303 against; on the KSSC/RSAR option the voting was 151 for and 206 against.)

1.32 Considerable efforts were made in the Committee Stage in the Lords to extend the category of exempt 'large shops', thus enabling the shops in question to open for longer than six hours. In particular, amendments were tabled to exempt DIY stores, garden centres, motor accessory shops, book shops, pet shops, farm shops and shops in leisure complexes.

1.33 The Bill was given a Third Reading in the House of Lords on 19 May 1994.

THE NEW ACT

1.34 The new Act itself remains very similar to the original SHRC option. Its purpose was to simplify enforcement, to give effective employment protection, and to liberalise shop opening on Sunday.

1.35 In the remaining Chapters of this book consideration is given as to whether these aims have been fulfilled and explanations are given of the likely difficulties of enforcement and other legal issues which result from the Bill as it has been enacted.

1.36 The Act received Royal Assent on 5 July 1994. The Act itself comes into effect by virtue of section 1 on the 'appointed day', being the day so appointed by the Secretary of State by statutory instrument. The appointed day is 26 August 1994 (SI 1994/1841).

2 What is a shop?

WHAT WAS A SHOP UNDER THE 1950 ACT?

2.1 The question raised by the title of this chapter has been the subject of on-going litigation throughout this century both in respect of the ban on Sunday trading contained in the Shops Act 1950 and in respect of the remainder of that Act insofar as it relates to the regulation of trading hours on weekdays. Three main issues arose under the 1950 Act.

What is a 'retail trade or business'?

2.2 The first issue which arose was that of the definition of a 'retail trade or business'. In particular, questions repeatedly arose under the Act as to whether this expression included service industries such as travel agents, estate agents, launderettes, and the repairers of goods and, more importantly in the last few years, whether it included shops which were open for the hire of goods only, in particular video hire shops.

2.3 The definition of a 'shop' contained in s 74(1) of the 1950 Act was—

'... save where the context otherwise requires—

"retail trade or business" includes the business of a barber or hairdresser, the sale of refreshments or intoxicating liquors, the business of lending books or periodicals when carried on for the purposes of gain, and retail sales by auction, but does not include the sale of programmes and catalogues and other similar sales at theatres and places of amusement;

"shop" includes any premises where any retail trade or business is carried on;'.

2.4 There was unanimous agreement that in this context 'trade' referred specifically to the activity of buying and selling goods. However, with regard to the expression 'retail business' there was substantial doubt as to the extent to which the use of these words determined whether premises were or were not a shop. Early cases[1] suggested that anything from which man profited was a business. The concept has proved difficult to enforce and the common understanding of the words has changed. As a result English and Scottish courts appear to have reached conflicting decisions on the meaning of the expression in the Act. The English courts have held that the business of a travel agent is not a retail trade or business,[2] whereas in Scotland for planning purposes travel agents were expressly brought within the meaning of that expression. Early decisions of the courts on what constituted a 'shop'[3] suggested that a shop was a place not only for selling but for storing, and that it has a structure or base as distinguished from a business carried on at a place. Thus at this stage historically, the position as to what was a shop depended on the difference in physical location and characteristics, and any litigation that occurred arose in connection with what was a retail trade (ie buying and selling) rather than any other type of economic activity.

---

[1] *Harris v Amery* (1865) LR 1 CP 148; *Smith v Anderson* (1880) 15 Ch D 247, CA.
[2] *Erewash Borough Council v Ilkeston Co-operative Society Ltd* (1988) 153 JP 141.
[3] See *Pope v Whalley* (1865) 6 B & S 303 and *Collman v Roberts* [1896] 1 QB 457.

2.5 What is a shop?

2.5 As the various new shop hours laws came into effect between 1892 and 1912, the definition of 'shop' gradually changed. The Shop Hours Act 1892 included market stalls and warehouses within the definition and did not make use of the concept 'retail trade or business'. The Shops Hours Act 1904 had a new definition, similar to that contained in the 1950 Act, namely—

> 'the expression "shop" includes any premises or place where a retail trade (including the business of a barber) is carried on'.

It is clear from this that at this stage the words 'or business' are missing from the definition.

2.6 From 1911 onwards the law was substantially strengthened to regulate the opening of shops. Acts were passed in 1911, 1912 and 1913, with the original purpose of the 1911 Act being, as previously explained, to include a prohibition on Sunday trading. For the first time there appeared in the 1911 Act the definition of 'shop' as 'includes any premises where any retail trade or business is carried on'. Thus there is an important drafting distinction between the use of the word 'means' in s 9 of the 1892 Act, and the use of the word 'includes' in s 14 of the 1911 Act.

2.7 The Home Office published a Memorandum in 1912, the objective of which was to state in plain language the provisions of the new code of law relating to shops contained in the 1912 Act. The second edition was published in 1913 to explain the provisions of both the 1912 and 1913 Acts. The memorandum recorded that the Law Officers had given advice on the interpretation of the Act. The first section dealt with the meaning of the word 'shop'. The memorandum explained that generally speaking a 'retail trade' was the sale of goods in small quantities to the public. It was then suggested that 'laundry receiving houses where articles are received to be cleaned, servants, registry offices, and places where articles are let for hire are not shops, unless articles are also sold on the premises'.

2.8 This was welcome news to the Automobile Association who had asked a parliamentary question in 1911 in order to be assured that the hiring of a car from a garage on a Sunday was not within the scope of the Act. The document was a very important one and by 1912, 100,000 copies had been sold.

2.9 The 1934 Volume of Halsbury's Laws of England[1] asserted that the business of hiring articles to the public did not constitute a business within the meaning of the Shops Acts and the note referred specifically to the two memoranda.

---

1 See Vol 14 2nd edn—published in 1934, note (o) on p 674.

2.10 The Home Secretary's view was stated by the Earl of Feversham in a debate[1] on a motion on 25 July 1935. He expressed the opinion that places where articles were let for hire were not shops unless articles were also sold on the premises. It was understood that local authorities held the same view at that stage.

---

1 HL Deb, 25 July 1935, col 868.

2.11 In 1936 a Bill was introduced in the House of Lords, at very much the same time as the Shops (Sunday Trading Restrictions) Act 1936 (see Chapter 1). The Shops

What was a shop under the 1950 Act? 2.16

Act 1936 received Royal Assent on 14 July 1936 and the Shops (Sunday Trading Restriction) Act 1936 on 31 July 1936. The purpose of the Shops Act 1936 was to bring 'the lending for reward of books and periodicals' within the definition of a 'retail trade or business' in the 1912 Act.

2.12 In *Lewis v Rogers*[1] the history is to some extent analysed in the judgment of Mann J at pp 7 and 8 of the transcript. It is clear that the court was not aware of the Home Office memoranda or the other material which is summarised above. Mann J explained his analysis that processors, cleaners and repairers of articles carried on a 'retail business' if they dealt directly with the public and he added hirers of articles to that list.

[1] *Lewis and Lewis v Rogers* (1984) 82 LGR 670.

2.13 As the above history shows, his view was most probably erroneous. It is absolutely clear that the Home Office, on the advice of the Law Officers and those sponsoring the 1936 legislation, knew that a lending library was not a shop within the meaning of the 1912 Act.

2.14 It has to be accepted, however, that the English courts took the option of classifying certain kinds of service businesses as retail businesses contrary to the expectation of the Law Officers when the legislation was passed. The landmark decision in this respect was that of the Court of Appeal in *Ritz Cleaners Ltd v West Middlesex Assessment Committee*.[1] The Court of Appeal held that cleaning services were in the nature of a 'retail trade or business' in that the work was brought to be done and taken away when completed by the customers without the intervention of a middleman and thus the property involved was a retail shop. Whether the premises were a shop in the context of other legislation was also considered in *M & F Frawley Ltd*.[2]

[1] *Ritz Cleaners Ltd v West Middlesex Assessment Committee* [1937] 2 KB 642, [1937] 2 All ER 368, a decision on the Rating and Valuation (Apportionment) Act 1928.
[2] *M & F Frawley Ltd v Ve-Ri-Best Manufacturing Company Ltd* [1953] 1 QB 318, [1953] 1 All ER 50, a case under the Leasehold Property (Temporary Provisions) Act 1951, s 10.

2.15 In the context of the Shops Act, a Divisional Court concluded in *Ilford Corp v Betterclean*[1] that a coin operated launderette was a shop within the meaning of the Act although it concluded that no offence had been committed because there was no personal service of customers. The Divisional Court did not think it necessary to decide the point but was inclined to accept the view expressed by the magistrates.

[1] *Ilford Corp v Betterclean (Seven Kings) Ltd* [1965] 2 QB 222, [1965] 1 All ER 900.

2.16 Perhaps the most important point of the decision in *Lewis v Rogers* is that the Divisional Court did not appear to have been made aware of the Scottish decision of the High Court of Justiciary which had rejected the English view as expressed in *Betterclean*. In *Boyd v A Bell & Sons*[1] the issue arose squarely for decision. Were premises where a dry cleaning business was carried on, with articles being accepted and returned clean to customers over a counter, a shop within the meaning of the Shops Act or not? The answer was that they were not. Lord Justice Clerk was against interpreting the Act

2.16 *What is a shop?*

to include the provision of services; Lord Wheatley regarded the extension of the Act to services as unwarranted, and Lord Walker favoured the narrower construction.

---

1   *Boyd v A Bell & Sons Ltd* (1969) SLT 156.

2.17 In *Lewis v Rogers*[1] Mann J said 'If a service is provided on premises which is fairly described as a retail service, that is to say, a service in regard to an article which is a service given to certain members of the general public in return for payment, then I regard the premises as being within the extended meaning of "shop"'.

---

1   [1984] 82 LGR 670.

2.18 In the *Erewash*[1] case the Divisional Court proceeded on the basis that *Lewis v Rogers* was correct, although the right was reserved for that decision to be challenged in the House of Lords. The travel agent in that case escaped on a number of grounds, including the fact that it was not carrying on the business of selling and that it was not concerned with goods.

---

1   *Erewash Borough Council v Ilkeston Co-operative Society Ltd* (1988) 153 JP 141.

2.19 In the circumstances, it appears highly arguable that the examination of the legislative and external history leads to the conclusion that the 1950 Act has been wrongly interpreted and has been extended to cover premises and types of businesses which those framing the original Shops Acts had no intention of so covering.[1] The issue is due back before the Divisional Court on appeal in the case of *South Tyneside Metropolitan Borough Council v Ritz Video Film Hire Ltd.*

---

1   *North West Leicestershire District Council v Gramlo Ltd*, (13 May 1988, unreported) judgment of the Court of Appeal.

What is 'retail'?

2.20 Secondly, the issue of what constituted a 'retail' trade or business became important with the growth in alternative forms of retailing. Shops which would historically have been described as wholesalers began to be used more frequently by ordinary consumers and the growth of the idea of retail clubs also became of importance.

2.21 'Retail' was generally believed to refer to transactions between an enterprise and a member or members of the public in quantities such as were appropriate to a transaction with the end user rather than a middleman.[1] A retail seller has been described as one who 'deals with consumers'. Such conceptions were perhaps clear at the early part of this century but over the last decade or so have become truly blurred. Many major DIY stores for instance sell substantial volumes of goods to traders, who purchase from DIY stores rather than builders merchants. In turn, such traders use the goods that they purchase as part of fulfilling contracts with their own customers. As such the DIY retailer is acting as a wholesaler.

---

1   See *Treacher & Co Ltd v Treacher* [1874] WN 4.

What was a shop under the 1950 Act? 2.26

2.22 This distinction has been further blurred by the arrival of retail clubs. This was illustrated by the recent decision of the High Court in connection with the American warehouse club Costco.¹ This case concerned a judicial review application by Tesco, Sainsbury and Safeway seeking to quash the planning permission granted to Costco by Thurrock Borough Council for a warehouse club for the sale of goods. The issue in question was whether in effect for planning purposes the operation of Costco was a retail operation or a club, which for purely commercial reasons excluded certain ordinary members of the public who wished merely to purchase a few small items. Costco's operation included charging members a subscription of somewhere in between $25 and $35. To be a member the customer must either be a business or within an employment group specified by Costco.

¹ *R v Thurrock Borough Council, ex p Tesco Stores plc* (1993) 137 Sol Jo LB 276.

2.23 In this case, the court was referred to *Lewis v Rogers* (see para 2.12) but discounted the issues raised there by pointing out that in *Lewis v Rogers* the club was a 'sham' to get around the Shops Act 1950 whereas in the Costco case, as pointed out previously, the scheme was entirely lawful and put together for sound commercial reasons. The judicial review application was unsuccessful.

What are premises?

2.24 Thirdly and finally the issue of what were 'premises' within the 1950 definition was also an on-going problem in connection with such enterprises as market stalls and mobile retail outlets.¹ This issue was partly hidden by the fact that the 1950 Act also extended the Sunday trading provisions to other places where retail trading took place.² Against this background the new definition of 'shop' in this Chapter is examined and the issues arising from it are considered.

¹ For examples of these issues see: *Dennis v Hutchinson* [1922] 1 KB 693 (stalls containing mechanical games not a 'shop'); *Eldorado Ice Cream Co Ltd v Clark* [1938] 1 KB 715 (warehouse depot and tricycle selling ice creams not a 'shop' or 'place'); *Summers v Roberts* [1944] KB 106, [1943] 2 All ER 757 (an uncovered market stall not a 'shop'); *Cowlairs Co-operative Society Ltd v Glasgow Corpn* 1957 JC 51 (a trailer van not a 'shop' but was carrying on a retail trade in a place other than a 'shop'); *Stone v Boreham* [1959] 1 QB 1, [1958] 2 All ER 715; *Greenwood v Whelan* [1967] 1 QB 396; [1967] 1 All ER 294 (fairly permanent stall not a 'shop' but a 'place'); *Maby Corpn v Warwick Borough Council* [1972] 2 QB 242, [1972] 2 All ER 1198 (a market stall used Saturday and Sunday only, not a 'shop' but a 'place'); *Randall v D Turner (Garages) Ltd* [1973] 3 All ER 369, [1973] 1 WLR 1052 (an exhibition stand was a 'place'); *Jarmain v Wetherell* [1977] 121 So Jo 153, (a coin and stamp fair held at a hotel not a 'shop' nor a 'place').
² Shops Act 1950, s 58 'The foregoing provisions of this part of this Act except ... shall extend to any place where any retail trade or business is carried on as if that place were a shop, and as if in relation to any such place the person by whom the retail trade or business is carried on were the occupier of a shop ...'.

2.25 As was explained in Chapter 1, the SHRC's proposals, which form the background to the new legislation, started upon the basis that small shops should be totally deregulated and that large shops should only be allowed to open for a limited time on Sundays. The proposals also proceeded upon the basis that trading otherwise than from 'shops' should not be the subject of regulation; thus for instance, there was no intention to legislate for market traders, car boot sales, occasional auctions or other sales held in hotels or other similar places.

2.26 It is also important to consider why the question of what is a 'shop' remains of importance. First, if the business in question is not 'a shop' within the meaning of the

11

2.26 *What is a shop?*

Sunday Trading Act 1994, it is clearly not obliged to comply with the provisions contained in any part of the 1994 Act save possibly those in Sch 4.

2.27 Thus, for example, for premises which may be greater than 280 sq metres and which would therefore have to limit opening to six hours on Sundays, such limitation will not apply if the premises in question are not a 'shop' within the meaning of the 1994 Act.

2.28 However, crucially, it should be noticed that the definition of a 'shop' for the purposes of regulating its opening hours under the new law is different from the definition of 'shop' when it comes to the giving of rights to shop workers in respect of Sunday working (see Chapter 11).

WHAT IS A SHOP FOR THE PURPOSES OF THE REGULATION OF SUNDAY OPENING HOURS UNDER THE 1994 ACT?

2.29 Schedule 1, para 1 provides that—

> '"shop" means any premises where there is carried on a trade or business consisting wholly or mainly of the sale of goods'.

In the same paragraph 'sale of goods . . .' is defined as *not* including—

> '(a) the sale of meals, refreshments or intoxicating liquor for consumption on the premises on which they are sold, or
>
> (b) the sale of meals or refreshments prepared to order for immediate consumption off those premises'.

The service sector and hirers of goods

2.30 As set out in para 2.29, the 1994 Act redefines the meaning of 'shop'. It is submitted that the service industries such as travel agents, estate agents, launderettes, and repairers of goods, are no longer covered by the definition and fall outside the provisions of the 1994 Act insofar as the regulation of trading hours is concerned.

2.31 Therefore the existing case law on this subject will be of no great relevance insofar as any alleged offences in respect of the regulation of Sunday trading hours is concerned save for deciding whether employees are 'shop workers' for employment protection purposes.

2.32 It will be a question of fact and law whether the trade or business of a shop consists 'wholly or mainly of the sale of goods'. The burden of proving that the premises are 'a shop' within the meaning of the definition would fall upon the prosecution and it appears that they would have to show that at least 50% of the turnover of the business consisted of sales as compared for instance with hire, repairs, cleaning or other such activities.

2.33 The expression 'wholly or mainly' was the subject of considerable debate[1] before the House of Lords during the passage of the Bill. That debate primarily

What is a shop for the purposes of the 1994 Act? 2.38

centred upon the use of the expression in connection with a number of debated exceptions to the six-hour opening period for large shops, but mention was made in the course of the debate of the use of the expression in the key definition of what constituted a 'shop' under the 1994 Act.

---

[1] By way of example see HL 3R, 19 May 1994, cols 419–429.

2.34 It is therefore necessary to consider what might be meant by the expression and how the courts have considered the expression in the past. It is necessary to start by making it clear that the expression 'wholly or mainly' is one frequently used by Parliamentary draftsmen.[1]

---

[1] For examples, see the Transport Act 1968, s 10(1)(xvii) and the Local Government (Miscellaneous Provisions) Act 1976, s 75(1)(c).

2.35 It is also an expression which the courts have had to face in many other contexts, but there is no precise and definitive statement as to its meaning. It is worth noting that the expression is used in the 1950 Act, s 18, although there are no recorded decisions on that provision.

2.36 However, there are helpful decisions specifically on the point of what is a 'shop' for the purposes of the Leasehold Property (Temporary Provisions) Act 1951. In s 20(1) of that Act, 'shop' was defined as being 'premises occupied wholly for business purposes, and so *occupied wholly or mainly* for the purposes of a retail trade or business' (author's emphasis).

2.37 The Court of Appeal dealt with two appeals specifically covering this expression.[1] In the first case, the court held that the test was to determine how much of the business done therein was retail business and not how much of the space comprised in the premises was used from time to time in the production of articles for retail sale. As a result of that test, premises used for a number of business activities, about 90% of which were wholesale and only 10% retail, were held not to be a 'shop'. In his leading judgment Sir Raymond Evershed MR stated that 'no doubt, the relative income gained by the different activities conducted on the premises is a *most important* (and, possibly, in some cases *the most important*) element for consideration but it is not necessarily exhaustive' (author's emphasis). In the second case, a dairy from which no milk was sold but which was used for housing spare bottles and a refrigerator and other articles in connection with the business of a milk roundsman was held not to be a 'shop'.

---

[1] *Berthelemy v Neale* [1952] 1 All ER 437 and *Deeble v Robinson* [1954] 1 QB 77, [1953] 2 All ER 1348.

2.38 The most recent decision relating to these words is *Fawcett Properties Ltd v Buckingham County Council*.[1] In that case, the words 'in industry mainly dependent upon agriculture' in a planning condition were analysed by the House of Lords. In his dissenting judgment Lord Morton said (at p 512)—

> 'The word "mainly" at once gives rise to difficulties. Probably it means "more than half" and this was the meaning which this House gave to the phrase "the bulk thereof" in *Bromley v Tryon* [1952] AC 265, [1951] 2 All

2.38 *What is a shop?*

ER 1058. Even so, one must ask "more than half of what?" ... Does the word refer (for instance) to turnover, to value or volume of goods produced for agriculture, to value or volume of raw material supplied by agriculture, or to profits? ... Moreover, all these factors may vary from time to time, and a business which is "mainly dependent" at one time may cease to be "mainly dependent" at another.'

---

[1] *Fawcett Properties Ltd v Buckingham County Council* [1961] AC 636, [1960] 3 All ER 503.

2.39 The suggestion raised in a number of House of Lords' debates that the formulation is unsatisfactory was roundly (and the author suggests correctly) rejected by Lord Hailsham who said that 'I am not at all worried by the words "or mainly". In this country the courts are judges of facts as well as of law.'[1]

---

[1] HL Committee, 14 April 1994, col 1657.

2.40 If the meaning of the expression were to be tested in the courts the author considers that the courts would be compelled to give the words 'or mainly' a wide interpretation, particularly since the question would be whether a criminal offence had been committed. In the author's view if the majority of the turnover on Sundays is on average attributable to the relevant types of sale, it would be extremely difficult for the prosecution to succeed. Other tests, such as one based on the number of transactions, might also be acceptable, although some (such as those based on the number of customers) are less attractive. The beneficiaries of the use of the expression are thus likely to be retailers, since some local authorities may well be reluctant to prosecute except in the most flagrant case.

2.41 In the light of this, it also seems clear that video hire shops as currently operated are unlikely to be 'shops' within the meaning of the new legislation and even if correctly decided the Divisional Court decision of *Lewis v Rogers* is in this respect no longer of importance (see para 2.12).

2.42 Similarly, much of the case law[1] interpreting the meaning of 'shop' and 'retail trade or business' under the 1950 Act can no longer be relied upon as being the correct interpretation of the new legislation on shop opening but it does remain of vital importance when interpreting the provisions as to shop worker protection, as to which see Chapter 11.

---

[1] See for instance, the cases referred to at para 2.4.

2.43 It appears likely therefore that the drafting of the new definition of 'shop' has successfully overcome many of the difficulties which existed under the 1950 Act in respect of the service industry sectors.

What is 'retail'?

2.44 The second problem highlighted above, namely what is 'retail', remained following the publication of the Bill in its original form. However, at Report Stage in the House of Commons[1] the Government brought forward an amendment specifically to deal with this issue and with the intention that traders who sold goods both to retail clients and to non-retail customers from a large shop were to be restricted on Sundays, to six hours trading with their retail customers.

[1] HC Report, 23 February 1994, col 328.

2.45 To do this, Sch 1, para 1 to the Bill was amended in a number of material ways. First, the word 'retail' was removed from the definition of a 'shop'. Secondly, two key definitions were inserted. Namely—

"'retail customer" means a person who purchases goods retail,

"retail sale" means any sale other than a sale for use or resale in the course of a trade or business . . .'.

These definitions are the key to overcoming the perceived problem. As will be seen later, an occupier of a large shop may only open it on Sundays for the serving of *retail* customers for a continuous period of six hours between 10.00am and 6.00pm.

2.46 The effect therefore of these key amendments is that all premises from which there is conducted wholly or mainly the trade or business of selling goods are now 'shops' within the meaning of the 1994 Act. Thus premises of wholesalers, cash-and-carries and retail clubs are 'shops' for this purpose. If they are small shops, they are totally free of restrictions but if they are large shops, then they may only open for 'retail sales' for the six-hour limit which is specified in the 1994 Act.

2.47 Undoubtedly from a practical point of view many of the types of shop in question will have difficulties devising a system which ensures that the customers to whom they are selling goods outside the six-hour period are 'retail' customers.

2.48 Many retailers historically sought to get round the provisions of the 1950 Act by selling to 'trade customers'. This usually involved some system of their trade customers being given cards and ensuring that no member of the general public who did not carry a card was entitled to enter those premises on Sundays. To obtain a card in many of these premises it was necessary to produce evidence that the customer was a trader or had a VAT registration number or that he was a director of a company or a sole trader or a partner of a trading business.

2.49 All of these methods were used to show that any sales to these people would be in the course of their trade or business and hence were not retail sale. However, the wording of the new statutory definition (see para 2.45) clearly shows that this will not be sufficient.

2.50 A member of a retail club for instance is more likely to be purchasing goods for his own use than for the use or resale in the course of a trade or business. In many cash-and-carries, despite the restrictions which these establishments have sought to be introduce, many sales are to people for their own use.

2.51 As a practical example, if a DIY store decided to open for longer than six hours but to restrict the sales of its goods to non-retail customers outside the six-hour period, it would appear that a sale to a builder attending a DIY store to purchase paint which he intended to resell to a customer would not be a retail sale and hence would be permitted. Similarly, if he was purchasing the paint to paint his own offices, this would be acceptable. If, however, he was to purchase the paint for the purposes

2.51 *What is a shop?*

of painting his own house, this would be a retail sale and hence would mean that the shop was open for the serving of retail customers outside the six-hour period.

2.52 As discussed later (see Chapter 10) the trader may be able to establish a defence of due diligence but in the author's view the systems for monitoring retail and wholesale trade operated by most major companies at the present time would not be sufficient for a due diligence defence to be made out. Such traders may be wise therefore to limit their opening hours to six hours only on Sundays.

2.53 In view of the very substantial maximum fine which can now be imposed by the courts, it seems unlikely that traders will take the risk of keeping their shop open for non-retail customers.

What are premises?

2.54 The third difficulty experienced under the 1950 Act was the identification of the sorts of 'premises' which fell within the restrictions either as shops or such other places where a retail trade or business was carried out. To an extent this issue continues to exist.

2.55 As is apparent from the definition of 'shop' set out earlier in this Chapter, it is apparent that a shop is defined as 'any premises'. Unfortunately, the Act contains no definition of what are 'premises' for the purposes of the Act.

2.56 Reference to other legislation[1] confirms that where the term is intended to have an expanded construction and to refer, for example, to land which adjoins a building, or even to aircraft, vessels, and the like, an interpretation is invariably provided. A practical problem relates to private forecourts, which abut but which do not form part of the highway. They are regularly used for trading purposes. Historically many such forecourts have been formed from the front gardens of private houses, which in their turn have been converted to business or retail use. Are such forecourts to be treated as a relevant part of the premises, albeit not comprised in the building, for the purposes of determining whether or not the area of the shop exceeds 280 sq metres? Will it make a difference if the forecourt in question is covered by an awning, or, as often occurs, a rigid roof and fixed side walls? Even if these areas are part of a 'shop' it is unlikely that this will affect the definition of whether a shop is, or is not, a 'large' one.[2] This is because, as will be discussed in Chapter 3, in deciding for the purposes of Sunday opening hours whether a shop is a large or small one, regard is to be had to 'internal floor area'.

---

[1] See eg the Private Places of Entertainment (Licensing) Act 1967, s 7(2) and the Trade Descriptions Act 1968, s 39(1).
[2] See Chapter 4.

2.57 Particular problems may arise in the case of markets. The fact that the definition does not refer to markets does not necessarily mean that they are not covered in the expression 'shop'. It is certainly arguable that the expression 'shop' is sufficiently wide to include both a permanent covered market (and indeed the individual stalls there) and also a temporary market (although possibly not the individual stalls). In the case of certain markets with shops, permanent stalls and temporary stalls, it may be that difficult questions will arise for which different answers will cover the case of different traders. A similar difficulty will be encountered in the case of car boot sales, for whereas each individual pitch might not be 'premises' the whole operation could be classified as a 'shop'

2.58 A further difficulty is whether telephone mail order businesses trading from office premises could lawfully be conducted on a Sunday outside the six hour period. Are such premises from which such a business is operated a 'shop', falling within the definition? First, it must be conceded that such offices are 'premises' within the definition. Secondly, these premises are used 'wholly or mainly' for retail sales to consumers. However, it is unlikely that courts would interpret the Act in this way because—
  (a) such an office would not be described in common parlance as a shop.
  (b) customers do not visit the premises to purchase goods and therefore this may not be a service of customers; and
  (c) there is no record of any suggestion that the 1950 Act applied to such premises, and as the definition of shop in that Act was wider than under the 1994 Act and as the latter is a liberalising measure, it seems unlikely that the court would extend the meaning of a 'shop' in this way.

2.59 It must be remembered however, that although this apparent lack of clarity may exist, in practice it is unlikely to be of great significance. It is only material in deciding whether the premises in question are a 'large shop' or not. If the premises are below 280 sq metres (as discussed in Chapter 3) they are totally exempt from any restrictions on Sunday trading. The only issue therefore is whether in these difficult areas of lack of clarity of the definition, large premises are restricted to six hours trading. In the case of many markets and car boot sales, it is unlikely that they will wish to exceed six hours from a trading point of view in any event. It is useful to remember that 90% of all shops in England and Wales fall under the 280 sq metre limit.

2.60 The most likely outcome is that the courts will interpret 'premises' for the purposes of this Act by reference to physical buildings, which are of a permanent nature. This is consistent with the idea of the definition of 'relevant floor area'.

2.61 As is explained in Chapter 11, the employment protection provisions of the Act cover a far larger group of workers than those who work merely within 'shops' as defined in Sch 1 to the Act and therefore the issue does not apply in the same way to the issue of who is a shop worker.

2.62 The operators of markets and car boot sales therefore who operate from inside a building should give consideration as to whether or not the operations are 'shops' and as to whether therefore they are obliged to restrict their trading hours to six hours and to give the appropriate notices to the local authority.

THOSE WHO ARE OR ARE NOT SHOPS

2.63 It appears therefore that the following are not 'shops' under the 1994 Act—
  (1) Estate agents.
  (2) Professional offices.
  (3) Banks/Building societies.
  (4) Launderettes.
  (5) Off licences.
  (6) Outdoor market stalls.
  (7) Outdoor car boot sales.

2.63 *What is a shop?*

      (8) Shops which primarily repair goods (shoe repairers).
      (9) Video hire shops.
     (10) Other hire shops.
     (11) Restaurants.
     (12) Public houses.
     (13) Mail order offices.
     (14) Travel agents.
     (15) Cafés.
     (16) Dry cleaners.
     (17) Wine bars.

2.64 The following probably are shops—
     (1) Indoor markets.
     (2) Indoor car boot sales.
     (3) Cash and carry.
     (4) Wholesale warehouses.
     (5) Retail clubs.
     (6) Catalogue shops.

OTHER DIFFICULT ISSUES

Shop in shops/concessions

2.65 The status of these types of businesses under the statutory scheme is difficult. Is a small shop situated in a large store allowed to open on Sunday for more than six hours even though the large shop is not? The answer must be found within the definition of 'shop' in the Act. The correct view, it is suggested, is that unless the public has direct access to the 'shop in shop' not through the main store and unless the 'shop in shop' is in a fully walled area making it distinct from the entirety of the main store, such a business is part of a 'shop' and not a 'shop' itself. A decision interpreting the definition in the 1950 Act supports this.[1]

---

[1] *Fine-Fare Ltd v Brighton County Borough Council* [1959] 1 All ER 476, [1959] 1 WLR 223.

In store cafés and restaurants

2.66 Stand-alone cafés, restaurants, take-away food shops, and public houses are not shops (see para 2.29). What is less clear is the position of such businesses when they are situated in a 'large shop'. May these parts of these shops open outside the six-hour period? Again it is suggested that, as in para 2.65, the physical layout and accessibility to the public may be the key to deciding whether the café is a separate shop. However, even if it is not, no offence may be committed (see Chapter 10).

Auctioneers

2.67 Auctioneers' sale rooms may also cause a difficulty under the Act. The actual area in which the auction is conducted may well be less than 280 sq metres, but what

Other difficult issues 2.68

of the area in which goods such as furniture are laid out for display before the auction? If this is taken into account in assessing the size of the shop, the premises may become a large shop and hence only be allowed to open for six hours on Sundays. This may be inconvenient for the auctioneer's requirements.

2.68 There is no doubt that auctioneers' premises are shops within the meaning of the Act. The trade or business of an auctioneer from his shop clearly consists 'wholly or mainly' of the sale of goods. From a practical point of view it may well be that the way round the apparent difficulty is by use of the mechanism for viewing only as to which see the full discussion contained in paras 4.6–4.16. On the other hand occasional auctions held from premises such as hotels will not change the nature of those premises because of the holding of such auction make them 'shops'.

3   Small shops

THE NEW PROVISIONS

3.1   As explained in Chapters 1 and 2 the basic scheme of the Sunday Trading Act 1994 is to allow all shops other than 'large shops' as defined in the Act to open without restriction on Sundays.

3.2   This is achieved by a series of definitions in Sch 1, para 1 and by s 5 of the 1994 Act which deals with the existing limitations on shop opening hours contained in the Shops Act 1950.

3.3   In this Chapter three issues are dealt with as follows—
    (a)   What is a small shop?
    (b)   How is the calculation of floor area carried out?
    (c)   What is the effect of s 5 of the Act?

WHAT IS A SMALL SHOP?

3.4   As explained in Chapter 2, it has become apparent that 'shops' for these purposes are limited to those premises where a trade or business is carried on consisting wholly or mainly of the sale of goods. The issue of whether such premises are not a 'large shop' for the purposes of the Act depends on the issue of what is the 'relevant floor area'.

3.5   The 1994 Act does not define a 'small shop' but does define a 'large shop' (Sch 1, para 1). A 'large shop' means—

> 'a shop which has a relevant floor area exceeding 280 square metres'.

For the purposes of this Chapter therefore any shop which has a floor area of 280 sq metres or less is described as a small shop.

3.6   In the consultation document published by the Government in July 1993 an area of 280 sq metres was illustrated as being the size of a singles tennis court.[1]

---

[1]   'Reforming the law on Sunday Trading—A Guide to the Options for Reform' (Cm 2300, July 1993).

HOW IS THE FLOOR AREA CALCULATED?

3.7   The relevant floor area for the purposes of deciding whether a shop is a 'large shop' or a 'small shop' means—

> 'the internal floor area of so much of the shop as consists of or is comprised in a building, but excluding any part of the shop which, throughout the week ending with the Sunday in question, is used neither for the serving of customers in connection with the sale of goods nor for the display of goods'.

How is the floor area calculated? 3.16

3.8 It becomes clear therefore that 'internal floor area' only is being considered and the issue of whether external areas of premises form part of the shop itself, which was discussed in Chapter 2, is not relevant for the purposes of doing the necessary calculation.

3.9 It is also apparent that only certain parts of the internal floor area of the shop need to be taken into account, namely those which are used either for the serving of customers in connection with the sale of goods or for the display of goods. In this respect it is necessary to comment on three issues.

3.10 First, the definition suggests that it is not satisfactory to look at the position of the relevant floor area on the Sunday in question but at the position as it has been for the previous week ending with that Sunday.

3.11 In marginal cases where stores are close to the 280 sq metre limit it is possible to envisage a situation where the layout of the store could change from time to time and this could have the effect of taking the store over or under the relevant floor area limit.

3.12 This provision, which involves looking at the position throughout the week, is clearly meant to prevent shops being able to open on Sundays merely by rearranging their layouts on Saturday night and restricting the area devoted to the serving of customers and the display of goods on Sundays. Thus the idea of large shops opening small areas of their stores on Sundays outside the six-hour period is clearly provided for and would be unlawful.

3.13 Secondly, it is necessary to consider what sort of areas within shops are used for the serving of customers in connection with the sale of goods? Clearly checkout areas, counters and aisles between gondolas used for displaying goods will all fall within this definition. Conversely it would appear that areas in shops set aside for restaurants, staff canteens, warehouse provision, offices and the entrance areas of stores are unlikely to be included within the relevant floor area.

3.14 The third issue relates to areas used for the display of goods. Clearly this includes all gondolas on which goods are displayed, shelving, certain counter areas, and areas in shop windows which are commonly used for the display of goods. Other areas such as window sills, alcoves and other similar areas in which goods are habitually displayed are likely also to be included within the relevant area although arguments may depend on the use of the word 'floor' throughout the section.

3.15 The main concerns about defining large and small shops by reference to floor size and the likelihood that this would cause difficulties in marginal cases are made worse by the fact that there is scope for argument and discussion as to what constitutes areas used for 'the serving of customers in connection with the sale of goods' and areas 'used ... for the display of goods'. In those circumstances unless the position is clear it seems unlikely that the prosecution will be able to show that the shop is a 'large shop' within the meaning of the Act.

3.16 However, because of the large penalty prescribed by this Act for breaches of the provisions relating to the opening of large shops, operators of stores which may or may not fall within the relevant floor area limit need to take particular care in deciding whether to open in excess of six hours. They need to give careful consideration to a due diligence defence to which reference is made in Chapter 10. In practice, however, it is thought unlikely that this is going to be a difficult problem.

3.17 *Small shops*

3.17 In addition, it is unclear how areas used for the display of goods which are displayed for hire rather than for sale are classified. In some entertainment shops, the business consists of the sale of videos and music (tapes, records, CDs) as well as video hire. These premises may be 'shops' because their turnover in sales of goods may exceed the turnover in hire. However, whether they are to count, in deciding whether they are a 'large shop' or a 'small shop', the area which is provided for the display of goods for hire is unclear. On the natural reading of the paragraph one would anticipate that the area is to be included in the calculation, but bearing in mind that the previous part of the definition referred to the 'serving of customers in connection with the sale of goods', an argument could be made out that the display of goods refers to goods which are available to the consumer for purchasing. In some stores this may be all important in deciding whether a shop is a large or a small one within the meaning of the Act.

3.18 Finally, what precisely is being measured when the 'internal floor area' is calculated? Is the internal floor of a building to be taken from the inside of the external walls or by measuring from the edge of the display gondolas which might be around the external walls? It appears likely that the intention is that measurements should be taken from the external wall area. For a small number of shops this may be material in deciding whether the shop is a large or a small one.

WHAT IS THE EFFECT OF S 5 OF THE ACT?

3.19 Having decided that as a matter of fact and law the premises in question are 'a shop' and fall below the relevant floor area for a large shop, then as a 'small shop' it is able to open on Sundays without restriction. This is achieved by s 5 of the Act which deals with the effects of Part I of the Shops Act 1950.

3.20 In fact, at the time of writing this book, the Deregulation and Contracting Out Bill, which is currently before Parliament, proposes the repeal of Part I of the 1950 Act.

3.21 Part I of the 1950 Act deals with early closing, general closing hours and supplemental provisions. Section 2 of the Act provides that shops shall close not later than 8.00pm in the evening and 9.00pm on the evening of the late day. The section uses the term 'day of the week' and has been interpreted as applying to Sundays as well as Monday to Saturday inclusive. There is no record of any prosecution being brought by a local authority under s 2 in respect of shops opening on Sundays after 8.00pm although many small shops, video hire shops and convenience shops in particular, have habitually opened after 8.00pm on Sundays for a substantial period of time. Whether it was possible to be charged both with an offence under the 1950 Act, s 47 (the prohibition on Sunday trading) and an offence under the 1950 Act, s 2 has never been litigated.

3.22 Against that background and to avoid any doubt on the issue, the Sunday Trading Act 1994, s 5(1) provides that Part I of the Shops Act 1950 'shall not apply on Sunday' and consequently the late day cannot be on a Sunday and the need to close at 8.00pm is overcome. The effect therefore of this amendment is that small shops need not close after the hour of 8.00pm in the evening on Sundays. There never has been a restriction on the time in which shops can open in the morning. Therefore small shops can open continuously from midnight on Saturday through to midnight on Sunday without any offence being committed.

4 Large shops

THE NEW SCHEME

4.1 The whole thrust of the Sunday Trading Act 1994 is to regulate large shops whilst completely deregulating small shops. As has been fully explained in the preceding Chapter, this is done by way of definitions as to what is meant by 'large shop' and how one calculates a large shop by reference to its relevant floor area.

4.2 Schedule 1, para 2(1) imposes a blanket prohibition on large shops opening on Sunday for the serving of retail customers in the following terms: 'subject to subparagraphs (2) and (3) below, a large shop shall not be open on Sunday for the serving of retail customers'.

4.3 As has been explained in Chapter 2 it is lawful to open for the serving of non-retail customers outside the six-hour period although the practical difficulties of doing so and the size of the penalties may make this an unwise course of action for most traders.

4.4 When considering the blanket ban it is important to note that as in the Shops Act 1950 the offence is keeping a large shop open on Sunday 'for the serving of retail customers'. It is necessary therefore to consider what is meant by this concept. It has been held on a number of occasions that the ban on Sunday trading contained in the 1950 Act, s 47 was a ban on 'the *personal* serving of customers'. Thus, it did not include the operation of a coin operated launderette on Sunday at which there were no staff in attendance other than the occasional attendance of a cleaner.[1]

---

[1] *Ilford Corpn v Betterclean (Seven Kings) Ltd* [1965] 2 QB 222, [1965] 1 All ER 900.

4.5 There are a number of cases relating to exposing cars for sale at garages on Sundays. In principle the mere exposing for sale does not constitute an offence under the 1950 Act, but other activities to assist customers such as taking them for a demonstration ride and engaging the customers in conversation on the merits of the vehicles in question and other such activities have all constituted a service of customers so as to constitute an offence under s 47[1]

---

[1] See eg, *Waterman v Wallasey Corpn; Hesketh v Wallasey Corpn* [1954] 2 All ER 187, [1954] 1 WLR 771 and *Monaco Garage Ltd v Watford Borough Council* [1967] 2 All ER 1291, [1967] 1 WLR 1069 and *Betta Cars Ltd v Ilford Corpn* (1959) 125 JP 19, 103 Sol Jo 834.

4.6 Many efforts have been made in the past to circumvent the ban contained in the 1950 Act in this respect and the most successful has been a system whereby stores are open for 'viewing only'. It has been held by the High Court that, if properly operated, there is no offence committed under s 47 of the 1950 Act if stores are open for this purpose.[1]

---

[1] *Yeovil District Council v DJB (Martock) Ltd*, (5 March 1982, unreported) judgment Chancery Division.

4.7 Large shops

4.7 In *Yeovil v Martock*, on application before Whitford J for an order that the defendant be committed for contempt arising out of an undertaking given not to open retail premises in Martock for the serving of customers on Sundays in contravention of the 1950 Act, the defendants justified their opening as opening for viewing only. The evidence showed that staff were in attendance with a notice that carpet fitting would be demonstrated on request. When the Shops Act Inspector visited the premises in the afternoon, he found four customers, and when he approached the proprietor he was told that he was not able to give information on a Sunday. The defendants provided leaflets for their customers on Sundays explaining how the system worked and there was a pull-off section at the bottom in which customers could ask for information. The store was advertised in the press as being open on Sundays for viewing and demonstration purposes only.

4.8 Whitford J indicated that the issue in question was whether or not as a matter of fact the defendant was serving members of the public. The Court concluded that the word 'serving' should be given its ordinary meaning, ie giving any form of assistance to another person. If, as in the particular case concerned, no information is given to the customer, then he is not being served. The serving of customers required by the Act meant that some form of assistance was to be given to them.

4.9 It is clear from the decided cases that there is a small distinction as to what constitutes a serving or not a serving of customers. Thus in *Betta Cars Ltd v Ilford Corpn*,[1] the appellants, who were car dealers, opened a garage on a Sunday and cars were placed on the forecourt. The cars had prices marked on them and notices relating to credit were exhibited. An employee was present and told the Shops Act Inspector that the shop was open for viewing only. In this case the Divisional Court held that the proposition that a shop could not be open for the service of customers unless a sale, or something approximating to a sale, took place, was not correct and that on the facts of the case, where goods were exhibited with prices and terms of sale and an employee was present, the Justices were right in convicting the appellants.

---

[1] *Betta Cars Ltd v Ilford Corpn* (1959) 124 JP 19, 103 Sol Jo 834.

4.10 Lord Parker CJ giving the leading judgment distinguished the facts in the *Betta Cars Ltd*[1] case from the facts of the earlier case of *Waterman v Wallasey Corpn*.

---

[1] Lord Parker said 'speaking for myself, I think it is an "entirely" position, namely, where the shop is lawfully open and a customer lawfully there for the purpose of the purchase of goods which can be sold that day. If he makes casual enquiries to some other commodity which will not be on sale until the next day, it seems to me it is very difficult to say that the shop is open for the sale of that commodity. That is quite a different case from the present case where the shop is not allowed to open for any purpose whatsoever yet goods are displayed and there are goods on the premises.'

4.11 The *Waterman* case was in fact two cases, one concerning a man called 'Waterman' and the other a man called 'Hesketh'. Both ran garages and both as part of the business of running garages sold motor accessories, petrol and oil which could be lawfully sold as they fell within the Fifth Schedule of the Act. Both could therefore keep their garages open for the transaction of sales in these commodities. Mr Waterman allowed a customer to inspect a car. No sale was effected and no money passed. In the *Hesketh* case the customer was given a trial run. In the *Hesketh* case the Court concluded there had been a serving of a customer, whilst in the *Waterman* case however there had not.

The exceptions 4.17

4.12 Another example is the case of the *Havering London Borough Council v Stone*.[1] The Divisional Court considered an allegation that the defendants had contravened the Shops Act 1950, s 2 by keeping its store open on a weekday past 8.00pm.

[1] *Havering London Borough Council v LF Stone & Son Ltd* (1973) 72 LGR 223.

4.13 In this case the defendants carried on the business of a department store and held an evening of hi-fi and stereo record demonstrations between 7.30 and 9.30pm. Admission was free to the public. Customers were given a programme and were able to look around the exhibition, view the equipment, which was priced, and listen to records. Three members of staff were present and representatives of the manufacturers were on hand to advise on and demonstrate the equipment, but no actual sales took place. The defendants were acquitted by the magistrates but on appeal, the Divisional Court held that it was an inescapable conclusion that all the activities which were carried on by or on behalf of the defendants showed a degree of repetition from which it could be said that the shop was open as a matter of business to promote sales from the shop. These activities came fairly and squarely within the ambit of 'the serving of customers'.

4.14 Taking all these cases into account, it is clear that what is or is not a personal serving of customers is a matter of fact but one where there may be fine distinctions. Whitford LJ in the *Yeovil v Martock* case did not seem to be prepared to follow Parker LJ's views in the *Betta Cars* case. He appreciated that the case before him was one in which the goods could not lawfully be sold on Sunday and concluded that he did not think the fact that people could view carpets to be bought the next day was sufficient for him to be able to say that the shop was open for trading on a Sunday in contravention of the 1950 Act. It was, he pointed out, common practice for shops to leave their lights on so that people could look through the window and see the goods on display. He could distinguish the case from *Betta Cars* as no information was given and no demonstration given. He concluded that the displaying of prices themselves was not sufficient to be a personal serving of customers.

4.15 Given the somewhat conflicting cases, it was usual for retailers to have large signs throughout their stores stating that no personal service could be given but that customers could purchase goods by completing order forms and leaving them for delivery on a week day, thus ensuring that no offence was committed.

4.16 Whether, following the enactment of this new law, any large shop will consider it helpful to be open outside of the six-hour period for the viewing of goods only, will have to be seen. Again in view of the risks of a much higher penalty and the fact that these stores will be able to sell goods for a continuous period of six hours it is perhaps unlikely (and unnecessary) that this will occur.

THE EXCEPTIONS

4.17 The three exceptions to the general ban on large shops opening on Sundays are to be found in the 1994 Act, Sch 1, para 2(2), (3). They are—
    (a) exempted shops (see Chapter 5);
    (b) shops occupied by those observing the Jewish Sabbath (see Chapter 8);

4.17 *Large shops*

(c) those who have given notice to the local authority of their opening pursuant to para 4 of Sch 1 (see paras 4.22–4.34).

4.18 However, even this latter exception does not apply to Easter Sunday or where Christmas Day falls on a Sunday. This ban on trading by large stores on Easter Day and Christmas Day was the only success of the KSSC in the course of the Bill before the House of Commons. The amendment in Sch 1, para 2(4) was moved by Mr David Alton and Mr Alan Beith and was adopted at Report Stage by 304 votes to 247.

WHO IS A RETAIL CUSTOMER?

4.19 The ban on large shops opening on Sundays is a ban limited to 'the service of retail customers'. The issue of who is a 'retail customer' and what is 'a retail sale' is set out in the 1994 Act, Sch 1, para 1 and has been discussed in detail at paras 2.44–2.53.

4.20 The issue of what constitutes 'the service of retail customers' as regards catering facilities within large stores needs to be considered. As discussed in Chapter 2 it is likely that such cafés and restaurants are not separate shops and hence will be part of large shops for the purpose of the control of opening hours. However, provided that the products sold are limited to 'meals, refreshments and intoxicating liquor', it appears that no offence is committed as there is no sale of goods (by reason of the definitions in Sch 1, para 1) and hence no 'service of retail customers'.

4.21 Stores who decide to keep their catering facilities open outside the six-hour period must ensure that a watertight system is in place to ensure that there are no sales or serving of customers with any product other than 'meals, refreshments or intoxicating liquor' so as to establish a due diligence defence. In addition, of course, arrangements must be made to ensure that the remainder of the store is out of bounds to customers!

THE NOTICE OF PROPOSED SUNDAY OPENING

4.22 If the occupier of a large shop or someone who has intentions of becoming such an occupier wishes to open that shop on Sunday then he must give notice to the local authority for the area in which the shop is situated.[1] That notice must state that the occupier proposes to open the shop on Sundays for the serving of retail customers and specify the six continuous hours beginning no earlier than 10.00am and ending no later than 6.00pm during which the store will open. These then become the permitted Sunday opening hours in relation to this shop. A notice may not take effect until the end of 14 days from the day on which it was given unless the local authority agree with the retailer that it shall take effect sooner.

---

[1] Sunday Trading Act 1994, s 1(1), Sch 1, para 4(1). See Appendix 2, Precedent 1.

4.23 Retailers and local authorities need to be careful about the timing of the service and effectiveness of notices upon the Act coming into effect. The difficulties in this respect have been noticed and Sch 1, para 9 now contains transitional provisions which

The notice of proposed Sunday opening 4.31

allow the service of the notice between the passing of the Act and before commencement notwithstanding of the provisions of Sch 1, para 4(3). Clearly, however, notice could not be given before the passing of the Act itself.

4.24 When the offences created by the Act are considered, the main offence is for a large shop to open outside of its permitted and notified Sunday opening hours. See further Chapter 10.

4.25 In the course of debates in the House of Commons, it was suggested that a shop which served such a notice was then obliged to open. This was disputed at the time by the Minister, who pointed out that the provisions of Sch 1, para 4(1) are enabling and not mandatory.

4.26 An argument could certainly be made that a notice which is served stating that the shop will open for example between 10.00am and 4.00pm should be cancelled if the shop has no current intention of opening. If a shop only wishes to open for four hours from 10.00am to 2.00pm or 2.00pm to 6.00pm, may it do so lawfully? The answer appears to be yes! Schedule 1, para 2(3) disapplies the blanket ban on large shops opening on Sunday for the serving of retail customers ('does not apply in relation to the shop during the permitted Sunday opening hours specified in the notice').

4.27 The notice provisions contained in Sch 1, para 4(1) must state by virtue of sub-para (b) 'a continuous period of six hours, beginning no earlier than 10 am and ending no later than 6 pm, as the permitted Sunday opening hours in relation to the shop'.

4.28 There is no obligation imposed on the shop actually to open during the permitted hours. Where there is a lack of clarity is that para 4(1)(a) provides that the notice should state that the retailer proposes to 'open the store on Sunday for the serving of retail customers'. If there is no intention to open in the immediate future, it could be argued that no notice should be served until that intention arises. However, in the case of an intention to open for only part of the permitted hours that argument clearly cannot apply.

4.29 Certainly para 4(2) provides that the occupier may at any time by a subsequent notice specify different permitted Sunday opening hours or cancel the earlier notice. It must be remembered that again such a notice will only take effect after 14 days.

4.30 There is a practical problem for certain retailers who may not open their stores every Sunday but will wish for instance to open for four or six weeks before or around the Christmas holiday period. Should such a retailer serve a notice which specifically relates to those Sundays? There is no specific provision in the Act which enables the retailer to do so but conversely there is no provision which prevents him from doing so. If he takes that course then it is arguable that he should not open on any other Sunday. Alternatively he might give a notice for instance in July by way of general notice of his intention to open on Sundays and not actually open until November. This may make the issue of enforcement more difficult for an enforcing authority.

4.31 A Precedent of a suitable notice giving the appropriate information is reproduced in Appendix 2, Precedent 1. This could be accompanied by a letter for the assistance of the authority explaining the likely Sundays on which the store will in fact open in the near future and if any part of the store such as the café or pharmacy, for example, will remain open outside the six-hour period.

4.32   *Large shops*

4.32   Once the notice has been given and has come into effect, then the retailer's only other duty is to display a notice pursuant to the terms of Sch 1, para 6. Such a notice need only be displayed when the shop is actually open for the serving of retail customers. The notice must specify the permitted Sunday opening hours specified in the notice served on the local authority and the notice must be displayed in a conspicuous position both inside and outside the shop.

4.33   Many stores already have displayed their store opening hours on purpose-built signs outside of the stores specifically for informing customers and these notices will be quite sufficient to comply with the retailer's duty as to external notices. Similarly, notices displayed on the store windows or properly displayed at the point of sale inside a store should be sufficient.

4.34   Notices are only required when the 'large shop' is open under Sch 1, para 2(3), ie it is open having given notice to the local authority. Notices do not have to be displayed by small shops nor by exempt shops, nor by premises which are not 'shops' for Sunday opening purposes, nor by shops to which the Jewish exemption applies.

5 Exempt shops

INTRODUCTION

5.1 As explained in Chapter 2, a number of shops which were previously covered by the Shops Act 1950 ban on Sunday trading have effectively become totally exempted as a result of the change in the definition of a 'shop'. It is worth remembering that shops in the service sector such as repair shops, launderettes, dry cleaners, estate agents, insurance companies and travel agents are no longer shops within the meaning of the Sunday Trading Act 1994 and therefore even if they are large (over 280 sq metres), do not have to comply with the six-hour opening provisions. Again it is necessary to remember that for the purposes of employment protection, their workers may well be 'shop workers' with all the new rights given in Sch 4 to the 1994 Act.

5.2 Secondly, the 1994 Act itself (see Sch 1, para 2(2)(a)) specifically exempts from the ban on Sunday opening a number of types of large shops, sometimes completely and sometimes for specific transactions only. These exemptions are contained in Sch 1, para 3. In this Chapter each of the exemptions is considered together with any difficulties which might surround its interpretation.

5.3 It seems clear that the purpose of the exemptions is to deal either with shops which were previously able to open lawfully on Sundays, or which of necessity should be able to remain open before or after the prescribed six-hour opening period for large shops.

PUBLIC HOUSES, OFF LICENCES AND TAKE-AWAY FOOD SHOPS

5.4 It was explained in notes on clauses for the Options Debate that the effect of the statutory definitions in Sch 1, para 1 to the 1994 Act, taken with the exemption contained in Sch 1, para 3(1) is that all public houses, restaurants, cafés and take-away food shops are exempt from the provision of the Act and are not therefore obliged to limit their opening to a six-hour period.

5.5 This is achieved in two ways. As previously mentioned, 'sale of goods' is defined so as not to include—
- '(a) the sale of meals, refreshments or intoxicating liquor for consumption on the premises on which they are sold, or
- (b) the sale of meals or refreshments prepared to order for immediate consumption off those premises'.

As to the meaning of 'meals or refreshments' see para 1.7. Schedule 1, para 3(1)(b) of the 1994 Act also exempts 'any shop where the trade or business carried on consists wholly or mainly of the sale of intoxicating liquor.'

5.6 Schedule 1, para 1 defines 'intoxicating liquor' as having the same meaning as in the Licensing Act 1964[1]. Thus public houses, restaurants and wine bars are dealt with by the exclusion referred to at para 5.5. Off licences are dealt with by virtue of a specific exemption at Sch 1, para 3(1)(b) (see paras 5.9–5.11).

5.6 Exempt shops

---

[1] 'Intoxicating liquor' means '. . . spirits, wine, beers, cider and any other fermented, distilled or spirituous liquor. . .' (Licensing Act 1964, s 201(1)).

5.7 By reason of the definition clause therefore it is clear that restaurants, cafés, public houses and wine bars are likely to be automatically excluded from the definition of a shop. Subject to the points mentioned below, the same applies to take-away foods shops.

Take-away food shops

5.8 Some learned observers of the drafting have commented on the provisions in respect of take-away food shops. They have suggested that the concept of '*immediate* consumption off the premises' (author's emphasis) may give rise to difficulty. Is the purchaser entitled to take his purchase home, perhaps to re-heat it in his own oven? Or ought he to consume it there and then on the pavement? If the restaurant provides facilities for consumption of the meal which has been ordered on the premises, subject to a different VAT treatment, which such a sale attracts, there ought in principle to be no distinction in legislative terms between the two transactions. There is also a point on the phrase 'prepared to order'. The customer who goes into the traditional fish and chip shop and asks the fish fryer behind the counter 'what is ready?' will be told what is on the drainer; and there will also be a quantity of chips available. None of the subsequent purchase of fish and chips has been individually prepared for the customer's order, but it is arguable that the *whole* parcel has been prepared to his order. Such critics had suggested a change in the wording of the clause.[1] The Home Office and the explanatory literature published with the Bill has made it clear that these criticisms have been rejected and that the existing provisions are properly drafted so as to exclude take-away food shops.

---

[1] See for instance, the Joint Opinions of Mr David Vaughan QC, Mr John Samuels QC, Mr Gerald Barling QC, Mr Nicholas Davidson QC, and Mr David Anderson—Commissioned by Hepherd Winstanley & Pugh entitled 'A Legal Review of the Draft Sunday Trading Bill', October 1993.

Off licences

5.9 By virtue of the 1994 Act, Sch 1, para 3(1)(b), off licences are also excluded. However by reason of the wording of para 3(1)(b) it is clear that off licences within, for instance, supermarkets are not excluded because their business is not 'wholly or mainly' the sale of intoxicating liquor. Such large shops therefore are obliged to obey the six-hour rule and are not allowed to open their off licence facilities outside that period.

5.10 The expression 'wholly or mainly' needs to be commented on. A full explanation of this expression and the issues surrounding it is to be found at para 2.32 ff. It is uncertain whether this expression requires an analysis on the basis of the number of transactions undertaken, the number of product lines, the number of customers, or the value of transactions, all of which would certainly lead to different answers. From an enforcement point of view this could give rise to considerable difficulties in the few isolated cases where large off licences appear to have a mixed business. One could perhaps envisage an off licence/convenience store which was a large shop within the meaning of the Act where it was not immediately apparent from a visual inspection what was going to be the main business of the shop.[1]

Public houses, off licences and take-away food shops 5.14

---
[1] For a more detailed discussion on 'wholly or mainly', see Chapter 2.

5.11 When considering defences in this matter in Chapter 10, consideration will be given to the sort of records which should perhaps be kept by retailers to maintain a due diligence defence in these extreme cases. The right of Inspectors to examine records, such as purchasing records, stock control records, VAT records, and till receipts may be vital to any prosecution of such a large off licence.

Chemist shops/pharmacies

5.12 Schedule 1, para 3(1)(d) refers to 'any shop which: (i) is a registered pharmacy, and (ii) is not open for the retail sale of any goods other than medicinal products and medical and surgical appliances'. A specific exemption has been given to large shops provided that they are registered pharmacies and are not open for the 'retail sale' of any goods other than 'medicinal and medical products and surgical appliances'. The definition 'retail sale' has been dealt with at para 2.44 ff. 'Medicinal products' and 'registered pharmacy' have the same meanings as those given to them in the Medicines Act 1968.[1]

---
[1] . . . '"medicinal product" means any substance or article (not being an instrument, apparatus or appliance) which is manufactured, sold, supplied, imported or exported for use wholly or mainly in either or both of the following ways, that is to say—
  (a) use by being administered to one or more human beings or animals for a medicinal purpose;
  (b) use, in circumstances to which this paragraph applies, as an ingredient in the preparation of a substance or article which is to be administered to one or more human beings or animals for a medicinal purpose.' (s 130).
'registered pharmacy' means 'premises for the time being entered in the register required to be kept under section 75 of this Act' (s 75) (see further Medicines Act 1968, ss 74, 75).

5.13 This provision is contained in the 1994 Act primarily to allow large chemist shops with over 280 sq metres of relevant floor area to open to fulfil their obligation to provide pharmacy services for prescriptions. The insertion of 'medical products' occurred at the Report Stage of the Bill in the House of Lords.[1] Its insertion was no doubt to deal with the suggestion that 'surgical appliances', which is not defined, would probably not include any surgical instrument or apparatus because the definition of 'medicinal products' treats appliances as being different from instruments or apparatus. Thus items probably included are those such as bandages and other surgical dressings which are expressly excluded from the definition of 'medical products' in the Medicines Act 1968. It still appears questionable, however, whether a large chemist shop should properly sell for instance a condom, outside the six-hour opening period, although they could probably supply oral contraceptives or a razor blade. It is understood that the major chemists in the country are satisfied, however, that the definition causes them no practical problems.

---
[1] HL Report, 5 May 1994, cols 1302–1304.

Airport shops

5.14 Schedule 1, para 3(1)(e) refers to 'any shop at a designated airport which is situated in a part of the airport to which sub-para (3) below applies'. The third type

5.14 *Exempt shops*

of shop specifically exempted is an airport shop by virtue of para 3(1)(e). To be exempted it must be situated at a designated airport and situated in part of the designated airport which is ordinarily used by persons travelling by air to and from the airport (see Sch 1, para 3(3)).

5.15 The purpose of the limitation in this specific provision appears to be to ensure that retailing units do not appear on designated airport land specifically to enable shops to open in excess of six hours on Sunday. The purpose of the exemption is to ensure that the requirements of the travelling public are met.

5.16 A 'designated airport' is given a specific meaning by Sch 1, para 3(4), namely an airport designated under an order made by the Secretary of State as being an airport at which there appears to him to be a substantial amount of international passenger traffic. Such power will be exercisable by statutory instrument and at the present time no such order has been made.

5.17 However, Sch 1, para 3(6) provides that any existing order under the Shops (Airports) Act 1962, s 1(2) (in force at the commencement of the Act, so far as it relates to England and Wales), shall have effect as if it were a designated airport under the said para 3(4) above and can be amended or revoked by order under that provision.[1]

---

[1] The present orders made under the Shops (Airports) Act 1962, s 1(2) are as follows—
'The provisions of Part I of the Shops Act 1950 (which relate to hours of closing) and of Part IV of that Act (which relates to Sunday trading) shall not apply—
(a) to any shop at a designated airport which is situated in a part of the airport to which this Act applies, or
(b) to the sale (otherwise than at a shop) of any goods at a designated airport, where the sale takes place in a part of the airport to which this Act applies, and is effected by or on behalf of a person carrying on a retail trade or business at a shop situated in such a part of the airport.'
The Orders relate to the following airports: Aberdeen, Birmingham, Edinburgh, Glasgow, Liverpool, London-Gatwick, London-Heathrow, Manchester International, Prestwick, Southend, London-Stanstead, East Midlands, Cardiff-Wales, Leeds/Bradford, Luton, Southampton, Bournemouth-Hurn, Humberside, Liverpool, Norwich, Tees-side, Exeter and London City.

Railway station shops

5.18 Schedule 1, para 3(1)(f) refers to 'any shop in a railway station'. This provision excludes 'any shop in a railway station'. Any large shop therefore in a railway station may open for as many hours as it requires on Sundays and is under no obligation to serve notices to that effect on the local authority. It appears unlikely there could be dispute as to what is a railway station although with the growth of retailing at stations such as Victoria the issue may arise. Provided the shop is within the curtilage of the station and on land owned or leased by the railway it appears to be exempt.

Service areas and petrol filling stations

5.19 Schedule 1, para 3(1)(g), (h) provides that any shop at a service area within the meaning of the Highways Act 1980 and any petrol filling station are similarly exempt.[1]

---

[1] A 'service area' is defined in the Highways Act 1980 as '... an area of land adjoining, or in the vicinity of, a special road, being an area in which there are, or are to be, provided service stations or other buildings or facilities to be used in connection with the use of the special road' (s 329).

Public houses, off licences and take-away food shops 5.25

5.20 As regards a petrol filling station it has been suggested that there might be a question as to 'what is a petrol filling station?'. If the objective of the exemption is (1) that a supermarket operator with a petrol filling station should not be entitled to open the supermarket except as a large shop for six hours, but the filling station section should be able to open without restriction, and (2) that the filling station with a small shop should be able to open both parts without restriction, then the exemption needed to be drafted as regarding the petrol filling station as itself being a separate entity.

5.21 The use of the word 'any' in Sch 1, para 3(1)(h) leads one to the conclusion that a petrol filling station, even on land owned and occupied by a major food retailer, is a separate shop for the purposes of the Act and if it is a large shop, it is exempted. Because it is a separate shop, however, this clearly means that the supermarket itself on the site is not a petrol filling station and cannot open outside the six hours.

Shops at ports and harbours and airport suppliers

5.22 Schedule 1, para 3(1)(j) refers to 'any shop which is not open for the retail sale of any goods other than food, stores or other necessaries required by any person for a vessel or aircraft on its arrival at, or immediately before its departure from, a port, harbour or airport'. The reason for this is less than clear. It may be that it is merely to replace the provisions of the 1950 Act, ss 56(1)(a), 65.[1]

---

[1] The Shops Act 1950, s 56(1)(a) provided that—
'Nothing in this Part of this Act shall prevent—
(a) the sale, dispatch or delivery of victuals, stores or other necessaries required by any person for a ship or aircraft on her arrival at, or immediately before her departure from, a port or aerodrome;'.
Section 65 provided that—
'Nothing in this Part of this Act shall prevent the sale, dispatch, or delivery of butchers' meat required by any person for a ship or aircraft on her arrival at, or immediately before her departure from, a port or aerodrome'.

5.23 The specific nature of the drafting raises a number of complex enforcement problems. How is the exemption to be understood, and why should it be restricted to 'on arrival, or immediately before departure'. For example, it could exclude the purchase of a shackle on a Sunday for routine maintenance on a boat, or for a voyage which was to start on Monday. More importantly perhaps, how can the enforcement authority regulate the exemption or prove that an offence has been committed?

5.24 Perhaps most surprisingly, however, given the exemption for airport shops, is the fact that there is no corresponding general exemption at ports or hoverports. Whether in practice, given the definition of 'shop' and 'internal floor area', this will cause difficulty is not yet clear.

Motor accessory shops

5.25 Schedule 1, para 3(1)(c) refers to—
'any shop where the trade or business carried on consists wholly or mainly of the sale of any one or more of the following—
(i) motor supplies and accessories, and
(ii) cycle supplies and accessories'.

5.26   Exempt shops

5.26 This was one of several amendments made by the House of Lords at Committee Stage or Report Stage to include further categories of exempt large shops. This amendment was supported by the motoring organisations and purported to replace the existing exemptions contained in the Shops Act 1950. The Fifth Schedule to the 1950 Act contained an exemption for the sales of motor supplies and accessories and cycle supplies and accessories.

5.27 The use of the words 'wholly or mainly' was criticised on a number of occasions in debates on this and other amendments, and the same comments which have been made previously at para 5.10 and in Chapter 2 apply here.[1]

---

[1]   For a more detailed discussion on 'wholly or mainly', see Chapter 2.

5.28 Without the expression 'wholly or mainly' retailers and enforcement agencies would have been involved in the difficult areas of deciding what are motor supplies or accessories. For a more detailed consideration of what is or is not a motor accessory within the similar provision contained in the Fifth Schedule to the Shops Act 1950 see para 1.7. The critics of the use of the wording 'wholly or mainly' complained that a large motor accessory shop could over the years change its product range so that although a substantial portion of its sales sufficient to bring it within the expression 'wholly or mainly' would be in motor accessories the other substantial portion could be in a completely conflicting product range.

5.29 This amendment along with nearly all of the other amendments which widen the exemptions were opposed by both those who supported the KSSC and those who supported the SHRC, because they sought to undermine the principle of the compromise which had been arrived at in the SHRC proposals. These arguments however were unsuccessful and many large stores (mainly out of town) in the non-food sector will as a result be able to open without restriction on Sundays.

Large farm shops

5.30 Schedule 1, para 3(1)(a) refers to 'any shop which is at a farm and where the trade or business carried on consists wholly or mainly of the sale of produce from that farm'. One of the other new exemptions introduced in the House of Lords was an exemption for large farm shops. It was said in the debate that there were over 100 farm shops whose internal floor area was greater than 280 sq metres and which had historically opened on Sundays for trade which they believed was lawful.

5.31 The existing provisions of the 1950 Act, whilst allowing sales of exempt produce listed in the Fifth Schedule, which included flowers, fruit and vegetables (including mushrooms) and fresh milk and cream (including clotted cream) had no specific provision for farm shops, save for a rather obscure provision in s 58 which provided that there should be added to the Fifth Schedule in respect of 'any sale at a farm, small holding, allotment or similar place, produce produced thereon'.

5.32 A number of short points need to be made about this rather surprising exemption. First of all the same issues which were raised and discussed in Chapter 2 concerning the expression 'wholly or mainly' should be considered. Secondly, the main products sold must be the produce of the farm in question. This may effectively mean that many large farm shops which it was intended should be able to open lawfully under this exemption may not be able to do so. How many large farm shops actually stock and sell over 50% of their turnover in home produced items? Thirdly, it is apparent that a shop which is set up to sell goods from more than one farm will fail the 'wholly or mainly' test unless it can show that over 50% of its turnover is generated from produce from the farm on which it is situated. Finally, it is clear that the shop must be 'at a farm' and presumably a shop situated away from the farm itself but which is owned by the farmer and sells 100% produce from his farm is not exempt.

Exhibition stands

5.33 Schedule 1, para 3(1)(k) of the 1994 Act refers to 'any stand used for the retail sale of goods during the course of an exhibition'. This was a further exemption moved and passed in the House of Lords which had the support of both the Government and the majority of local authorities. Schedule 1, para 1 (the definition provisions) has a definition of 'stand' as meaning in relation to an exhibition—

'any platform, structure, space or other area provided for exhibition purposes'.

The purpose of this exemption is clearly to enable exhibition stands at events where the stand area may well exceed 280 sq metres, such as a boat show or motor show, to operate lawfully on a Sunday outside the six-hour period.

Failed exemptions

5.34 In the House of Lords further attempts were made to exempt other large shops and in particular efforts to exempt totally—
(a) any shop which is a nursery, garden centre or do-it-yourself home improvement shop, or combination of these, and where the trade or business carried on consists wholly or mainly of the sale of any one or more of the following: (i) plants (ii) garden supplies and accessories and (iii) materials or tools suitable for the use in the construction, maintenance, repair or decoration of buildings;[1]
(b) any shop which is not open for the sale of any goods other than books, audio books and book tokens (or a number of variations thereon);[2]
(c) any shop within a holiday park and open only for the sale of goods as an incidental facility to paying guests using or enjoying other facilities at that park; (and other variations thereon);[3] and
(d) any shop where the trade or business consists of the sale of pets and pet supplies;[4]

were all defeated.

[1] HL Commons Amendments, 30 June 1994, col 925.
[2] HL 3R, 19 May 1994, col 433.
[3] HL 3R, 19 May 1994, col 440.
[4] HL Report, 5 May 1994, col 1248.

General issues for exempt shops

5.35 First of all it should be made clear that in respect of motor supply shops, off licences and farm shops Sch 1, para 3(2) makes it clear that in determining whether a

5.35 *Exempt shops*

shop falls within the exemptions regard shall be had as to the nature of the weekday trade as well as the Sunday trade. Clearly this is intended to ensure that a shop cannot escape the six-hour provisions by changing its product range and mode of operation on a Sunday only so that it is different from that which occurs during the week.

Video hirers and other hirers

5.36 As explained in Chapter 2, shops which open primarily for the hire of goods are no longer 'shops' within the meaning of the Act. As previously discussed, however, there may be certain shops whose main business is actually the sale of goods, despite the fact that a substantial portion of their business is the hire of goods, and which as such are 'shops' and if they are 'large shops' they are only able to open for six hours on Sundays. This is of special importance to certain leisure shops which feature both music and video sales and hire.

5.37 Can such shops and others who both hire and sell goods open lawfully outside of the six-hour period for the hire of goods only? It is suggested that they can. The offence created by the 1994 Act as previously explained is contained in Sch 1, para 2(1), namely that a 'large shop shall not be open on Sunday for the serving of retail customers'.

5.38 As the serving of retail customers is clearly defined in Sch 1, para 1 by reference to the words 'sale' and 'purchase', it can therefore be quite clearly shown that opening a shop purely for the hire of goods outside of the six-hour period cannot be an offence under Sch 1, para 2(1).

5.39 In the circumstances described in para 5.36 of a shop opening outside the six-hour period for the hire of goods only, or in connection with certain other of the exemptions, for instance the opening of a large pharmacy for the sale of all of its products for the six-hour period but outside of the six-hour period only in accordance with the exemption, the question arises as to the obligation of the retailer to serve notice on the local authority of its intended opening hours.

5.40 As a general rule, it is clear that a large shop which is totally exempt does not have to serve a notice on the local authority that it will be opening for six hours only. However, for this limited category of shops it appears that for the purposes of selling their total product range during the six-hour period, they are obliged to give notice to the local authority under Sch 1, para 4 of the 1994 Act. It may be sensible when giving such notice to make it clear to the local authority that the store will remain open outside of the six-hour period for an exempt purpose only.

6 The loading and unloading of lorries at large shops

THE BACKGROUND

6.1 One of the controversial areas surrounding Sunday trading, especially in respect of large stores in urban areas, is the alleged environmental impact caused by the movement of large lorries in the course of loading and unloading at stores on Sundays, particularly in the early morning. Following the clear intention of Parliament to liberalise Sunday trading in this Act, this issue gained more importance because it became apparent that for the purposes of delivering fresh produce to their stores on Sundays, food supermarkets would feel obliged to allow the loading and unloading of lorries on Sundays before the stores opened at 10.00am.

6.2 As a result this issue was raised at Committee Stage in the House of Commons and at Report Stage[1] the Home Office tabled specific provisions to deal with this problem. These provisions are contained in s 2 of, and Sch 3 to, the 1994 Act.

---

[1] HC Report, 23 February 1994, col 283.

6.3 Following consultation with local authorities and retailers, further provisions were introduced and amendments made at Report Stage in the House of Lords.

6.4 These powers are of course in addition to those which local authorities already have in order to control the loading and unloading of vehicles through planning permissions, or under the Highways Act 1980, other local Acts, and environmental legislation.

LOADING CONTROL AREAS

6.5 Section 2 and Sch 3 set up a new type of control by allowing local authorities to designate their area as a 'loading control area' for the purposes of the 1994 Act. Unfortunately, the Act only allows a local authority to designate its whole area and gives it no power to designate only part of their area. Thus local authorities will be forced to decide whether difficulties in one small locality in their area create sufficient justification for imposing restrictions throughout their area.

6.6 The procedure set out in the Act is relatively simple. A local authority may by resolution designate its area as a loading control area with effect from a date specified in that resolution. That resolution must specify a date at least one month after the date on which it is passed. Before making such a designation, the local authority is obliged to consult widely. Section 2(3) imposes a duty 'to consult persons appearing to the local authority to be likely to be affected by the proposed designation or revocation'.

6.7 As examples of this the Act suggests that occupiers of shops or local residents or their representatives will need to be consulted. Bearing in mind the fact (see para 6.5),

6.7 *The loading and unloading of lorries at large shops*

that a control area will be the whole area of the local authority this element of consultation may be very substantial.

6.8 Section 2(4) obliges the local authority to publish notice of the designation in a manner which, it considers appropriate. Once the loading control area comes into force, then the provisions of Sch 3 apply.

6.9 If it appears that until a local authority has amended its delegation scheme so as to delegate its rights and duties under the Act to a specific committee or officer of the authority, the whole Council will be obliged to pass such a resolution.

THE EFFECT OF A LOADING CONTROL AREA

6.10 Once the loading control area comes into effect then the occupier of a large shop which opens on Sundays may not load or unload or permit other persons to load or unload goods from a vehicle at the shop before 9.00am on a Sunday.

6.11 For this purpose a 'large shop' has the meaning described in Chapter 4. However, the restrictions on loading only apply to large shops which open pursuant to the 1994 Act, Sch 1, para 4, ie having served a notice on the local authority of their intention to open and specifying their permitted opening hours. The restrictions do not apply to large exempt shops. Therefore a large food supermarket in a loading control area is obliged to comply with the restrictions on loading and unloading whereas the adjoining motor accessory store which is opening as an exempt shop has no obligation to comply and may freely load and unload on a Sunday.

6.12 Should the occupier of a large shop covered by the restriction require deliveries before 9.00am on a Sunday then he may only do so with the consent of the local authority and then only in accordance with any conditions which are laid down in that consent.

6.13 To apply for permission to unload before 9.00am a retailer must make an application in writing. At the present time it is unclear what local authorities will require by way of information but the 1994 Act, Sch 3, para 4 makes it clear that the local authority can require such information as may be reasonable.

6.14 It may be reasonable to expect that a local authority will require information as to when it is anticipated the deliveries in question will be made, how many such deliveries will be made, what vehicles will be used in connection with the delivery, how the loading or unloading will take place, whether this will be with or without the aid of a mechanical device and how many employees will be involved.

6.15 In addition, a local authority may insist that a retailer pays 'a reasonable fee' in respect of the application. Despite representations made to the Home Office, no guidelines are set out in the Act as to what will be reasonable. Many fear that this is an issue which will lead to disputes between local authorities and retailers. Schedule 3 gives no guidance as to how the local authority will set its charges nor what costs the charges should seek to cover. A specific amendment limiting the charge to cover the administration costs of the local authority was withdrawn after debate at Third Reading in the House of Lords. However Lord Ferrers, responding for the

Government in that debate, made it clear that the change can only relate and be used to cover the *costs of processing the application* (author's emphasis).[1]

---

[1] See HL 3R 19.5.1994, col 442 and see also the Local Government (Miscellaneous Provisions) Act 1982, Sch 3, para 1(a) (sex shops) and the Noise and Statutory Nuisance Act 1993, Sch 2, para 5 (loudspeakers in the street) for examples of the use of this wording.

6.16 Retailers may be well advised to accompany their application with any evidence they have that no annoyance has been caused in the past or is likely to be caused in the future by their delivery pattern. It may also be sensible to provide the information which the retailer anticipates the local authority will require.

6.17 Once the application has been properly made, and presumably any additional information requested by the local authority has been provided, then Sch 3, para 6(1) lays down the local authority's duties and responsibilities. The local authority has a clear statutory duty to grant consent unless it is satisfied that such loading before 9.00am on Sundays 'has caused, or would be likely to cause, undue annoyance to local residents'.

6.18 Following the amendment of the 1994 Act in the House of Lords, the local authority has no duty to consult persons residing in the vicinity of the shop to which the application relates. Bearing in mind, however, that the local authority clearly has a duty to grant consent unless it is satisfied that annoyance is going to be caused to the local residents, it appears likely that it will be obliged to consult to ascertain this. If it fails to do so any refusal or grant of an application may well be the subject of a successful judicial review application by an aggrieved retailer.

6.19 The local authority is given powers by para 3(1) of Sch 3 to impose such conditions as it considers appropriate to any consent which it grants. Again, it would be difficult for it to impose conditions unless it has had the opportunity of considering the type of annoyance which is likely to be caused to local residents by consulting them. The very wide power given to local authorities may still be controlled by judicial review should it seek to impose conditions which are out of proportion to the alleged annoyance to local residents.

6.20 The local authority is given a very strict timetable within which to work. Schedule 3, para 6(2) imposes a duty on the local authority to determine the application and notify the applicant in writing of the decision within 21 days beginning with the day on which it receives the application. It must be assumed that an application will be taken to have been received only when it is complete and should the local authority require further information then the application will not be deemed to have been received until all the required information has been provided. This is an area which may also give cause for disagreement between retailers and local authorities. Where a consent is granted, the notification will also set out the conditions which are to be attached.

6.21 Schedule 3, para 8 provides that the local authority must, upon granting a consent, cause a notice giving details of that consent to be published in a local newspaper circulating in its area. This provision for publication is different from the duty contained in s 2 in respect of advertising the designation of a loading control area or the revocation of such an order.

6.22 *The loading and unloading of lorries at large shops*

6.22 If consent is granted subject to conditions, then what sort of conditions may properly be imposed? Such conditions may well concern where vehicles may be parked and unloaded, the earliest hour in which vehicles can arrive and be unloaded, provisions as to the idling of engines, the use of lifts, trailers and forklift trucks, the behaviour of employees, and other practical solutions to resolve noise problems.

THE REVOCATION OF A LOADING CONTROL AREA RESOLUTION

6.23 Section 2 of the 1994 Act contains identical provisions for the revocation of an order as those for the making of one. Hence, any resolution must take effect from a date at least one month from the date in which the resolution is passed. The local authority has the same duty before revoking an order to consult the same group of people as they would consult in making the order. Similarly, a local authority has the same duty to publish notice of the revocation in the manner it considers appropriate.

THE REVOCATION OF CONSENT GRANTED TO A RETAILER TO LOAD OR UNLOAD BEFORE 9.00AM

6.24 Schedule 3, paras 3(2), 7(a), (b) of the 1994 Act allow a local authority either to vary the conditions subject to which a consent has been granted or to revoke the consent entirely.

6.25 In the case of a variation, the local authority must give notice of the variation to the person to whom the consent was granted. It must be presumed that before any variation is made, a local authority should give consideration to the same issues as it would have considered when granting consent, subject to conditions at the time of the original application.

6.26 If an occupier of a shop in respect of which a consent is in force is convicted of an offence under Sch 3, para 9 by reason of his failure to comply with the conditions subject to which the consent was granted, then the local authority may revoke the consent.

6.27 Similarly, the local authority may revoke the consent if it is satisfied that the loading or unloading authorised by virtue of a consent has caused undue annoyance to local residents. In both cases the local authority has no duty to revoke but it may revoke at its discretion.

6.28 In the second case it seems clear that for a local authority to properly carry out its duty and properly exercise its discretion it will again have to consider all of the issues that it would have considered when the application was originally granted and will have to consult both with the retailer involved and with the local residents before it can fairly revoke. It should also consider whether its objectives can properly be achieved by the imposition or variation of the conditions imposed to the consent rather than its revocation.

APPEALS

6.29 The 1994 Act lays down no statutory appeal provisions either for the making or revoking of a designation of an area as a loading control area nor of the granting, refusal to grant, granting subject to conditions, or the revoking of a consent to load or unload pursuant to Sch 3.

OFFENCES

6.30 An occupier of a large shop, which is opening pursuant to Sch 1, para 4 of the 1994 Act (ie for six hours pursuant to a notice to a local authority), commits an offence in a loading control area if he loads or unloads or permits any other person to load or unload goods from a vehicle at a shop before 9.00am.

6.31 The person committing such an offence is liable on summary conviction to a fine not exceeding level 3 on the standard scale (currently £1,000).

6.32 By virtue of Sch 3, para 2, it is also an offence if the occupier allows loading or unloading, or permits any other person to load or unload goods from a vehicle at the shop before 9.00am in breach of any conditions which were imposed when consent was granted. For a full discussion of the offences created by the 1994 Act and the possible defences thereto, see Chapter 10.

7 Property law considerations

KEEP OPEN CLAUSES

7.1 As the result of representations made at Committee Stage[1] by Glenda Jackson MP (who was representing the views of a property lawyer resident within her constituency), s 3 of the Sunday Trading Act 1994 was inserted by the Minister at Report Stage.

---

[1] HC Report, 23 February 1994, col 299.

7.2 Landlords commonly require tenants of retail premises to accept either an obligation in their leases that they will keep those premises open for trade during usual business hours (or provisions of a similar nature). Such clauses are especially prevalent in leases of shops in shopping centres and can be of particular importance to landlords where they require an anchor tenant to be the mainstay of the centre until it is well established.

7.3 In these cases an existing provision in a lease or other agreement as to occupation could have the effect of requiring an occupier to keep open their premises for the serving of retail customers during normal business hours or during other hours determined by someone other than that occupier. The purpose of s 3 of the 1994 Act is to ensure that this should not be regarded as requiring or enabling that person to require, the occupier to open the shop on Sunday. This will clearly protect any occupier opening from Monday to Saturday in the usual way.

7.4 Furthermore, it may be that the provision, referring as it does to 'the occupier' may not properly address the issue. Any lease or agreement will require a 'tenant' or 'licensee', as opposed to an 'occupier', to keep the shop open for the serving of customers. A tenant would enjoy the benefit of the section if the lease contained the appropriate 'keep open' clause but the tenant may not in all cases be the occupier. If a tenant were to sub-let or otherwise permit occupation of its shop by a third party, that third party would be the occupier. Whilst most occupiers would in such circumstances be contractually obliged by the tenant to observe and perform the terms of its head lease and would thus enjoy the benefit of the section, this may not always be the case. Leases will, for example, permit tenants to allow companies within the same group of companies as the tenant to occupy the premises. In such circumstances, it could be that the group company occupying the premises would not be able to claim the relief of s 3 as it would not be the party 'required' by the lease to keep open the premises.

7.5 In addition, it has been suggested by some commentators that the effect of s 3 is unclear on clauses in leases where the lease has subsequently been assigned or the freehold interest subsequently sold so that there is no longer privity of contract between the original contracting parties. However, as between the respective successors in title, the terms of the lease will still be enforceable and it is thought that any tenant occupier would still have the benefit of the s 3 protection.

7.6 Whilst 'keep open' clauses in shopping centres are common, and no doubt shopping centre management teams will be keen to promote the success of their

Keep open clauses 7.10

centre by encouraging Sunday opening, it is considered extremely unusual for any lease of a shopping centre within the UK to have stated specifically that trading on a Sunday would be required. That being the case, the practical effect of s 3(2) will be very limited. Section 3(2) provides that the exception set out in s 3(1) does not apply where there is a specific provision in the lease relating to Sunday opening which requires trading on a Sunday which is lawful under the Shops Act 1950, Pt IV. For example, a motor accessories shop might well fall within such a category and an occupier of that shop could, as a result of s 3(2) still be required to open on Sundays pursuant to the terms of its lease if that lease specifically requires it to open on Sundays. This would be a clear cut case where the whole range of goods sold from the shop fell within the Fifth Schedule to the 1950 Act. But historically one of the principal difficulties of the interpretation of Part IV of the 1950 Act was in the area of mixed retailing. For instance, most of the major food supermarkets have been advised by their lawyers that up to 70% of their stock could lawfully be sold on Sundays as the goods fell within the exemptions contained in the Fifth Schedule to the 1950 Act. If the provisions of s 3(2) are applied to a lease of such a food superstore which expressly requires Sunday trading, some trade would undoubtedly be lawful whilst the sale of other goods would be unlawful. Whilst these issues remain unclear, it is expected that the courts will do their best to ensure that retailers are not obliged to open on Sundays unless the existing provisions of the lease were so clear on the subject under s 3(2) as to leave no doubt in the mind of the court.

7.7 Retailers at the cutting edge of retailing over the last few years have, together with their lawyers, been trying to ensure that landlords cannot prevent them from trading on Sundays as opposed to being required to trade on Sundays. Most institutional landlords have been happy to accept this subject to a full indemnity from the tenant where the local authority either takes or threatens to take action against the landlord for breaches of the 1950 Act. Most tenant's solicitors will have been well aware of the restrictions of the 1950 Act and will have vigorously opposed any imposition of a requirement to trade on Sundays by any landlord at the negotiation stage. Most institutional landlords also will not have not wished to have been seen to be actively promoting Sunday trading. For any landlord now to endeavour to attempt to enforce a covenant which has the effect of requiring Sunday opening would certainly be a case of gamekeeper turned poacher.

7.8 In any event, it is considered that it would be unusual for a tenant to be required by a court to actually keep premises open for trade and the question of damages for breach of covenant is a more realistic remedy.

7.9 In the event of a breach of usual Monday to Saturday opening covenants, it may well be that s 3 could be used to limit any claim for damages if it was sought to extend the effect of closure on a seven day as opposed to a six day opening week.

7.10 To date there has not been a move to apply for specific performance for tenants to keep premises open in accordance with a 'keep open' covenant but rather a move for damages for breach of the same.[1] Such being the case, it would be a new move for landlords to start seeking specific performance of leases to require trading on a Sunday. In the event of a tenant ceasing to trade altogether, it is thought that the effect or otherwise of s 3 would be somewhat academic.

---

[1] See *Transworld Land Co Ltd v J Sainsbury plc* [1990] 2 EGLR 255.

7.11   *Property law considerations*

SERVICE CHARGES

7.11   Despite many efforts in the House of Lords to bring in statutory provisions to cover the effect of Sunday trading on service charges, these amendments were all defeated or withdrawn. The real fear expressed was that shops which did not open on Sundays in a shopping centre where shops were open, would be subject to paying a proportion of the service charge, which related wholly to Sunday.

7.12   By reason of the failure of these amendments the parties will have to fall back on the contractual arrangements in existing leases. These need careful checking by all parties, the landlord before incurring expense and the tenant before paying!

OTHER ISSUES

7.13   Certain commentators have argued about the effect of the Act on rent review provisions of existing leases. It appears that in most cases, when the Act comes into force, a landlord will not be able to obtain an increase in rent from a tenant who is already trading on Sundays illegally because the tenant will be breaking a clause in the lease.

7.14   Because Sunday trading is sure to be demand led it is suggested there is a danger of a two tier rental market depending on the profitability of Sunday trading for the tenant. It is suggested that this will make the issue of comparables very complicated.

8 The Jewish exemption

THE BACKGROUND

8.1 The Jewish exemption is contained in the Sunday Trading Act 1994, Sch 1, para 2(2)(b) and Sch 2, Pt II. The background to the exemption is an historical one. At the time of the passage of the Shops Act 1936, which was ultimately consolidated into the Shops Act 1950, much Parliamentary time was spent debating the right of the Jewish minority, especially those in London, to close their shops on the Jewish Sabbath and in return have the right to open for some or all of Sunday. Ultimately such Jewish shopkeepers were given the right by s 53 of the 1950 Act in certain circumstances to open their stores on Sundays until 2.00pm.

8.2 Many practitioners in this area found the operation of s 53 difficult. Many applications were made by practising Jews under the provisions of s 53 to the Board of Deputies of British Jews and many applications were dismissed to the considerable upset of the applicants concerned. Despite efforts in the House of Lords for the exemptions to be further modernised, so as to ensure that all who believed in the Jewish Sabbath and were prepared to swear to that effect should merely have to inform the local authority by statutory declaration that this was the case. In return they could open their large shops outside of the six-hour period laid down by this Act. These amendments were defeated.

8.3 The new provisions enacted are of relevance under the new Act only in connection with the six-hour opening provision in respect of large shops. Substantial amendment to the procedure under the Act has been put through following an amendment at Report Stage in the House of Commons.[1] However, the control exercised by the Board of Deputies of British Jews over those of the Jewish religion remain.

---

[1] HC Report, 23 February 1994, col 369.

8.4 However, the issues which arose historically about the provisions of s 53 and in particular its relevance to market operators are unlikely to arise in the future because this provision is now only material in connection with the opening of large shops.[1]

---

[1] For the difficulties experienced about the operation of markets by those allegedly of the Jewish faith, see for instance *Thanet District Council v Ninedrive Ltd*, [1978] 1 All ER 703 in which an injunction was given to restrain *Ninedrive* operating a Sunday market pending the determination of their appeal against refusal to register them as persons of the Jewish faith; *Chichester District Council v Flockglen Ltd* (1977) 122 Sol Jo 61 in which the Court held that the whole market site was not to be treated as a 'place' pursuant to the Shops Act, s 58, but each stall had to be treated as an individual shop or place and the occupier himself had to apply for registration. On the same subject see also *North West Leicestershire District Council v Gramlo Ltd* (13 May 1988, unreported), in which the Court of Appeal refused to make a declaration that should the market operator be successful in its application for registration under s 53 the market could lawfully be operated from the land in question.

THE NEW PROVISIONS

8.5 The procedure for a person of the Jewish religion who wishes to open his 'large shop' on Sundays outside the six-hour period has been considerably simplified as a

8.5 The Jewish exemption

result of the amendments. The appropriate provisions are contained in the 1994 Act, Sch 2, para 9. Their effect is to provide a further exemption to the absolute ban on Sunday trading contained in Sch 1, para 2(1) (see Sch 1, para 2(2)(b)).

8.6 The procedure is now relatively simple. Any person of the Jewish religion who wishes to open a large shop on Sundays outside the six-hour provision gives a notice to the relevant local authority stating that he is a person of the Jewish religion and that he intends to keep the shop closed for the serving of customers on the Jewish Sabbath (Saturday). In the case of a partnership or a company, it is provided that if the majority of the partners or directors are of the Jewish religion, then such a notice may also be given.

8.7 Such a notice has to be accompanied by a certificate signed by an authorised person that the person giving the notice is indeed a person of the Jewish religion. In the case of a partnership or a company such certificate will be given in respect of each of the persons by whom a notice has been given, ie by the majority of the partners or directors.

8.8 An authorised person who may give such a certificate is defined in Sch 2, para 8(12) as either—
  (a) the Minister of the synagogue of which the person concerned is a member; or
  (b) the Secretary of that synagogue;[1] or
  (c) any person nominated for the purposes of this paragraph by the President of the London Committee of Deputies of British Jews. This Committee is usually known as the Board of Deputies of British Jews.

---

[1] Secretary of the Synagogue has the meaning contained in the Marriage Act 1949, Pt IV, namely—
  '(a) a person whom the President of the London Committee of Deputies of the British Jews certifies in writing to the Registrar General to be the secretary of a synagogue in England of persons professing the Jewish religion;
  (b) the person whom twenty householders professing the Jewish religion and being members of the West London Synagogue of British Jews certify in writing to the Registrar General to be the secretary of that Synagogue;
  (c) the person whom twenty householders professing the Jewish religion and being members of the Liberal Jewish Synagogue, St John's Wood, certify in writing to the Registrar General to be the secretary of that Synagogue;
  (d) a person whom the secretary of either the West London Synagogue of British Jews or the Liberal Jewish Synagogue, St John's Wood, certifies in writing to be the secretary of some other synagogue of not less than twenty householders professing the Jewish religion, being a synagogue which is connected with the said West London Synagogue or with the said Liberal Jewish Synagogue, St John's Wood, as the case may be, and has been established for not less than one year;'.

8.9 As in the 1950 Act, Sch 2, para 9 of the 1994 Act also accepts that other religious bodies observe the Jewish Sabbath. In respect of such other religions, the appropriate certificate is given by the Minister of the religious body concerned.

8.10 To save bureaucracy pursuant to the transitional provisions contained in Sch 2, para 10(1), (2), any shop which is currently registered under s 53 the 1950 Act shall be taken as having given the appropriate notice, and reference to a certificate shall include reference to the statutory declaration previously required under s 53(2) of the 1950 Act.

8.11 If the occupier of a large shop for which notice under these provisions has been served changes, or if the composition of a partnership or company changes then, unless a new notice is served, the old notice is deemed 'cancelled' at the expiry of 14 days from when the change took place (Sch 2, para 8(7) of the 1994 Act).

8.12 The effect of the provisions set out in para 8.11 is that upon the expiry of 14 days Sch 1, para 2(1) of the 1994 Act applies and the opening of the shop therefore becomes unlawful, an offence being committed under Sch 1, paras 2(1), 7(1).

8.13 As to other offences relating to the provisions of the 1994 Act, Sch 2, Pt II, see Chapter 10. By reason of those provisions, those of the Jewish religion or those believing in the Jewish Sabbath, who keep their stores closed for the serving of customers on the Jewish Sabbath are now entitled to open their stores on Sundays throughout the whole of that day without restriction. This is clearly substantially less discriminatory than the previous provision and is to be welcomed.

8.14 A precedent for a suitable notice under the 1994 Act, Sch 2, para 8(1), (4) is contained in Appendix 2, Precedent 2.

CANCELLATION

8.15 The occupier of the shop in question may at any time cancel the notice given in respect of his shop. The right to have the notice so cancelled is absolute and the local authority must cancel it on application being made by the occupier.

8.16 As previously mentioned at para 8.11, the notice will automatically be cancelled at the end of a period of 14 days from the date when there is a change in the occupation of the shop or in the composition of the partnership or directors of the occupying partnership or company.

8.17 Any person convicted of an offence under this part of the 1994 Act (as to which see Chapter 10) faces the fact that the local authority may cancel a notice under Sch 2, para 8(11). The power to cancel is absolute and could be only challenged by way of judicial review for being *Wednesbury* unreasonable.[1]

---

[1] *Associated Provincial Picture Houses Ltd v Wednesbury Corpn* [1948] 1 KB 223, CA.

9 The duties and powers of local authorities

BACKGROUND

9.1 In this Chapter all the provisions of the Act imposing duties or giving powers to local authorities are listed, and if not explained elsewhere, are examined in detail. Where necessary these duties and powers are compared with those under the Shops Act 1950 so that the material differences can be identified and understood.

WHAT IS A LOCAL AUTHORITY?

9.2 The Sunday Trading Act 1994, s 8 gives a statutory definition of the meaning of 'local authority' wherever it appears throughout the Act. A local authority means either—
- (a) a unitary authority; or
- (b) any district council which is not a unitary authority.

9.3 Section 8(2) defines 'unitary authority' as meaning—
- (a) the council of a county provided that within that county there are no district councils;
- (b) the council of any district provided that in the area there is no county council;
- (c) a London borough council;
- (d) a county borough council (but only from 1 April 1996);
- (e) the common council of the City of London; or
- (f) the council of the Isles of Scilly.

9.4 Therefore until the establishment of unitary authorities the local authority under the 1994 Act will be the same as the enforcement authority under the Shops Act 1950.

DUTIES OF LOCAL AUTHORITIES

Sunday opening—duty to maintain a register of large shops

9.5 Schedule 1, para 5(1)–(3) of the 1994 Act spells out the duties of the local authority in respect of shops which are large shops and are open for six hours on Sundays having given notice to the authority.

9.6 First, the local authority has a duty to maintain a register of shops in respect of which a notice under Sch 1, para 4 (the notice setting out the opening hours of that large shop) has effect. By para 5(3)(b) this record may be kept by means of a computer. For the ease of the local authority the notice to the local authority which appears in Appendix 2, Precedent 6, follows the order in which the particulars set out appear.

9.7   Those particulars which must be in the register are—
   (a) the name (if any) and address of the shop; and
   (b) the permitted Sunday opening hours specified in the notice.

The register maintained by the local authority must be open to inspection by the members of the public at all reasonable times.

The duty to enforce the Act

9.8   The local authority has a duty to enforce the Act within its area. This duty is set out in Sch 2, para 1 in the following terms—

> 'It shall be the duty of every local authority to enforce within their area the provisions of Schedules 1 and 3 of this Act and Part II of this Schedule.'

9.9   This duty is expressed in terms similar to most of the modern duties imposed on local authorities to enforce criminal provisions[1] but it is limited to the duty to enforce the restrictions on Sunday trading, loading control orders and the Jewish exemption.

---

[1] See for example the Trade Descriptions Act 1968, s 26(1), the Fire Precautions Act 1971, s 18(1), the Protection from Eviction Act 1977, s 6, the Consumer Protection Act 1987, s 27(1). For examples of statutes under which local authorities may wish to enforce, but which require consent of the Attorney General before the Prosecution can be instituted see the Prevention of Oil Pollution Act 1971, s 19(1)(a) and the Public Order Act 1936, as amended by the Race Relations Act 1976, s 71(2).

9.10   The duty to enforce contained in the Act is materially different from the duty imposed by the 1950 Act, s 71. That section read—

> 'It shall be the duty of every local authority to enforce within their district the provisions of this Act ..., and for that purpose to institute and carry on such proceedings in respect of contraventions of the said provisions ... as may be necessary *to secure observance* thereof' (author's emphasis).

The necessity for local authorities to take action 'to secure observance' placed a particularly onerous duty on them and as a result the duty has been the subject of much litigation over the past ten years.

9.11   A number of issues arose. First, could a local authority refuse to carry out its duties by reason of the fact that it had insufficient resources to enable it to do so? Secondly, was a local authority entitled when carrying out its duties to target first of all major retailers who broke the law on Sunday trading? Did the position outlined above change if in fact the local authority had no intention or no real intention of enforcing against the other retailers in their area who opened on Sundays?

9.12   What was the extent of the duty? Was it sufficient merely for a local authority to warn or prosecute or were they obliged to take out injunction proceedings, if despite prosecution retailers remained open and trading on Sundays in breach of the Act? Despite the change in the wording of the duty many of these issues remain of importance under the new Act.

9.13   In practice the duty to enforce should be far less onerous. It was reliably estimated that over the last few years around 120,000 shops regularly opened in

9.13 *The duties and powers of local authorities*

England and Wales on Sundays and nearly all sold goods which fell outside the authorised range. Many local authorities were faced with over 200 shops in their areas which were opened in such a way and in some areas the numbers were over 500. Given the resources of local authorities, the problems of obtaining the evidence necessary to prosecute to secure observance, and the fact that the majority of the local population most probably were opposed to the enforcement of the Act, the position became intolerable for the local authorities.

9.14 However, under the 1994 Act, local authority enforcement duties are going to be considerably reduced. All small shops can open without restriction and there are, as previously discussed, a number of exemptions to the ban on large shops opening. In effect it appears that it will be the local authority's duty to ensure that large shops only open for six hours on Sundays.

9.15 This duty will have a number of components. Local authorities will have to ensure that a store which is not immediately obvious as being either a small or a large one and which is open for more than six hours is in fact a small shop and thus entitled to open outside the six hour period. In this respect, it is hoped that local authorities will be realistic and sensible as to their duty and will not consider it necessary to carry out large scale measuring exercises throughout their area. Secondly, local authorities will have to ensure that large shops having notified their six hours do in fact only open for the notified period.

9.16 Local authorities will also need to ensure that the shops which are not classified as 'shops' but which open both for retail and non retail sales do only open for six hours for retail trade. This may require some inspection and understanding of the systems of retail clubs, cash-and-carries, and warehouse facilities in situations where it is clear that they are visited by retail customers as well as wholesale customers.

9.17 Local authorities may consider it necessary in cases where it is not immediately apparent that a shop is exempt, to carry out enquiries, using their powers which are described at para 9.43 ff, to ensure that they are satisfied that the shop is truly exempt either as not being a 'shop' at all, or under one of the statutory exemptions. This may, for example, mean forming a reasonable opinion following consultation with the retailer concerned as to whether or not the shop can comply with the 'wholly or mainly' test which might apply to that particular exemption.

9.18 Once the law becomes fully understood it is thought unlikely that many of these issues are going to result in the widespread disobedience of the law which has been experienced ever since the Shops Act 1936 came into force.

9.19 However the duty of the local authority is clearly an important one and the understanding of the duty under the provisions of the 1950 Act is important. For that reason the major case law on the subject is reviewed in this part of the Chapter.

9.20 In considering the extent of the duty upon the local authority under the 1950 Act it was clear that s 71 did not just give the authority *power* to institute and carry on proceedings: there is also a *duty* to enforce and a further duty to take such proceedings necessary to secure observance.[1] It has already been explained that the duty to take proceedings necessary to secure observance no longer appears in the 1994 Act.

---

[1] See Donaldson LJ in *R v Braintree District Council, Ex Parte Willingham* (1982) 81 LGR 70 at 72.

9.21 The decision of the Court of Appeal in the first *Stoke v B & Q* case[1] is an important guide as to how that duty is to be performed. The Court recognised in that case that 'failure to secure observance of the Act tends to generate complaints of unlawful and unfair competition by traders who do not comply with it' and indicated that disgruntled traders could apply for 'mandamus' to force the authority to take action. It could be added that discriminatory enforcement tends to generate complaints from those against whom the Act was enforced in that they faced unfair competition from those who opened on Sundays but against whom the Council chose not to enforce the Act.

[1] *Stoke-on-Trent City Council v B & Q (Retail) Ltd* [1983] 2 All ER 787, CA.

9.22 Ackner LJ gave the most specific guidance as to how a local authority should approach its task under s 71 of the 1950 Act—

'This section unequivocally obliges the local authority to use the best means they can, having regard to their resources, "to secure observance" of, inter alia, s 47 of the 1950 Act.'[1]

[1] See para 9.21.

9.23 Later in his judgment he reiterated the fact that the duty was subject to the local authority's resources and set out how that duty could then be fulfilled. He suggested that the appropriate steps to take should be a warning, followed by prosecution, followed ultimately by an injunction.

9.24 In the same case in the House of Lords[1], Lord Roskill appeared to qualify the effect of Ackner LJ's comments by saying—

'My Lords, I see no reason why when considering whether it is necessary to institute and carry on proceedings, the local authority are not entitled to have regard, in relation to the particular case or cases in question, to the financial consequences of any suggested action. If for example there is a serious or doubtful question of law involved which may involve a series of appeals and thus cast a heavy financial burden on ratepayers, whatever the result but especially if the prosecution ultimately fails, I cannot think that the local authority after taking proper legal advice is debarred from taking that fact among others into account before reaching their final decision whether or not it is necessary to institute and carry on proceedings.'

Both Lord Diplock and Lord Fraser agreed with this statement.

[1] *Stoke-on-Trent City Council v B & Q (Retail) Ltd* [1984] 2 All ER 332, HL.

9.25 It is important to note that Lord Roskill was commenting on passages from the judgment of Donaldson LJ in the *Braintree* case and was saying that Donaldson LJ's remarks might be interpreted unduly widely when he said that expense is irrelevant to the question of whether to enforce, although potentially relevant to the decision how to do so.

9.26 *The duties and powers of local authorities*

9.26 From the above cases it would appear that the courts would avoid saying that local authorities' resources are altogether irrelevant to the decision whether to enforce and institute proceedings even in a situation where it is clear that positive action is needed to secure observance by a particular retailer.

9.27 The House of Lords in *Kirklees v Wickes*[1] expressly decided that a situation can arise in which the duty under s 71 extends to a local authority's decision under the Local Government Act 1972, s 222 to seek an injunction.

---

[1] See *Kirklees Metropolitan Borough Council v Wickes Building Supplies Ltd* [1992] 3 WLR 170.

9.28 Taking all these matters into account and considering the new section imposing the statutory duty on local authorities to enforce the 1994 Act, it appears that they will be left less open to any action for a mandamus to compel them to take steps to enforce the Act. However, the issue of discriminatory enforcement remains. It appears from the *Stoke v B & Q* case that local authorities may properly enforce by picking on a few retailers with a view to making an example of them.

9.29 But what of a local authority who decides, as many have in the past, to respond only to advertising of unlawful Sunday trading or certain types of complaints.

9.30 It has been argued in the past that this sort of policy must be unlawful because it overlooked the duty contained in the 1950 Act, s 71(2), now contained in Sch 2, para 2 of the 1994 Act, to appoint Inspectors to carry out the statutory duty. It has been argued that this duty to appoint Inspectors who have the wide powers referred to later in this Chapter (para 9.43 ff) together with the duty to enforce suggests that the authority must not merely respond to circumstances in which a breach of the Act is notified but must enquire for itself whether the Act is being observed. The proposition that a Council can permanently abandon any pro-active approach appears to be wrong.

9.31 It also appears that a local authority which acquiesces in the breach, although it might find it more difficult to secure enforcement by way of injunction, cannot be criticised for enforcing the law thereafter.[1] In the *South Somerset* case there was no evidence that the defendant acted to its detriment and the Divisional Court gave very short shrift to the notion that it was a legitimate expectation and one which the Court should protect that the plaintiff would continue to refuse to carry out its duty to enforce the law.

---

[1] See *R v South Somerset District Council Ex parte DJB (Group) Ltd* (1989) 153 LG Rev 813.

9.32 Many of these issues were considered by the Divisional Court on 27 July 1993 in *Tesco Stores plc v Kirklees MBC* (McCowan LJ and Leonard J) (unreported). In that case the Divisional Court declined to carry out a judicial review of a decision by the local authority to embark on considering enforcement proceedings by way of civil proceedings for an injunction. The thrust of the application was that Kirklees MBC had adopted an unlawful enforcement policy and that they had resolved only to enforce Sunday trading provisions of the 1950 Act against major retailers and not against small traders. Although, contrary to the assumption which had been made by Tescos, it appeared on late evidence that Kirklees MBC were attempting to enforce the Act uniformly the Court did accept that universal enforcement of the Act in Kirklees was impracticable. The implications of the judgment of the Divisional Court appeared to be that if the local authority failed to take all reasonable steps to enforce s 47 across the board, then it would be open to criticism that it was acting unlawfully and hence its enforcement policy could be the subject of a judicial review. A selective enforcement policy may therefore be unlawful, although in this case the Divisional Court did make it clear that even if they had considered the policy adopted by the particular local authority was unlawful, they would have been reluctant to have granted relief to a retailer which was itself open in that area or throughout the country in breach of the provisions of the statute. Clearly this will remain the situation under the 1994 Act and it is unlikely that a retailer will be able to successfully judicially review a policy of enforcement of the local authority when it is itself in persistent breach of the criminal law.

9.33 In conclusion, therefore, whilst it is clear that a local authority remains under a statutory duty to enforce the Act, the removal of the requirement that its duty extends to 'securing compliance' means that it will be less susceptible to action taken against it by retailers or other local inhabitants seeking to ensure that it enforces the Act whether by prosecution or injunction. In any event it appears unlikely that retailers who are open and seek to judicially review an enforcement policy of the local authority are likely to have much sympathy from the Divisional Court.

9.34 Before leaving this subject it is worth commenting upon whether it is necessary to raise the issues of the unreasonableness of the authorities' enforcement policy by way of judicial review or whether, as an alternative, by way of defence in injunction proceedings. In the first *Stoke* case, the House of Lords was explicit about this.

> 'Section 222 of [the 1972 Act] requires that a local authority shall only act if they "consider it expedient for the promotion or protection of the interests of the inhabitants of their area".[1] Any exercise by the local authority of this statutory power is subject to the control of judicial review and the applications of the principles enunciated in [*Wednesbury*]. In considering the exercise of its powers the local authority must take into account matters which it ought to take into account, ignore matters which it ought not to take into account and then reach a decision which a reasonable local authority could have arrived at. Where the local authority seeks an injunction, the Court will consider whether the powers have been rightly exercised and whether the discretionary remedy of an injunction should be granted, taking into account all the circumstances at the date the application for an injunction is considered by the court' (per Templeman LJ).[2]

[1] Local Government Act 1972, s 222.
[2] *Stoke on Trent City Council v B & Q (Retail) Ltd* [1984] 1 AC 754.

9.35 This appears to be the clearest statement by the highest authority that when the Court is considering an application for an injunction it will consider, if asked to do so, in accordance with the *Wednesbury* principles, whether the decision under s 222 is a proper one.

9.36 Unfortunately the Court of Appeal in a later case (not relating to Sunday trading),[1] appears to have decided that an attack on a local authority's decision under

9.36 The duties and powers of local authorities

s 222 can only be made in judicial review proceedings, unless the challenge is 'in support of a private law right' which as a general rule is unlikely. This is a particularly unfortunate decision, since the Court of Appeal was not referred to the first *Stoke* case. It approved of the earlier decision of Scott J.[2] The *Stoke* case was cited and it appears that the passage from the *Stoke* case which is referred to in para 9.34 was not cited to Scott J.

---

[1] *Avon County Council v Buscott and Others* [1988] 1 QB 656.
[2] *Waverley Borough Council v Hilden and Others* [1988] 1 WLR 246.

9.37 This issue is important because local authorities have contended in the past that the court is not entitled to consider the validity of a decision under s 222 of a local authority unless judicial review proceedings are launched. Whether or not that contention is wrong, it is one which will no doubt have to be faced by retailers in such situations.

9.38 From a practical point of view it may be that the simplest way round this is to issue judicial review proceedings and to seek leave to have those judicial review proceedings heard at the same time as an application by the local authority for an interlocutory injunction to restrain a breach of the 1994 Act.

Duty to appoint inspectors

9.39 Schedule 2, para 2 of the 1994 Act imposes a duty on the local authority to appoint Inspectors to carry out their statutory duty. This provision mirrors the 1950 Act, s 71(2).

Duties under the Jewish exemption

9.40 Schedule 2, Pt II, which establishes the Jewish exemption, has been dealt with in detail in Chapter 8. However, the duties imposed on local authorities by that part of the Act are again highlighted.

9.41 Schedule 2, para 8(5) imposes a duty on the local authority to keep a register containing particulars of the name (if any) and address of every shop in respect of which a notice has been served telling the local authority of the intention of the occupier to keep his shop closed for the serving of customers on the Jewish Sabbath. Any register under the paragraph must by virtue of para 8(6) be maintained for inspection by a member of the public at all reasonable times and may be kept on a computer.

Duties relating to loading control areas

9.42 The provisions contained in Sch 3 which relate to loading control areas have been dealt with in Chapter 6. Local authorities have a number of duties under the provisions of Sch 3 and s 2. A local authority has a duty to dispose of any application for consent within 21 days of receiving it (see Sch 2 para 6(2)). The local authority has a duty, before making or revoking a designation of an area as a loading control area, to consult persons appearing likely to be affected by the proposed designation or revocation. For detailed provisions, see Chapter 6.

POWERS OF LOCAL AUTHORITIES

9.43 Local authorities are given a number of powers in order to support the duty of the local authority to enforce the Act.

9.44 For the purposes of supporting their duty to enforce, Inspectors appointed by local authorities have a number of specific powers under Sch 2, para 3. These can be exercised subject to two conditions—
    (a) that if required, the Inspector produces duly authenticated documents showing his authority; and
    (b) that the powers are exercised at reasonable hours.

9.45 Subject to these two conditions an Inspector may enter any premises within his local authority area. If necessary he can be accompanied by a police constable but he is not required to be so accompanied. He may enter premises solely for the purpose of finding out whether there is or has been *on those premises* any contravention of the provisions of the Act. Thus he cannot enter the head office of a retailer under these powers to investigate a contravention in the company's store elsewhere.

9.46 The Inspector may require the production of and inspect and take copies of, any records relating to any business conducted on the premises. He is entitled to those records in whatever form they are held, but he is only entitled to them if they appear to him to be relevant for the purposes of ascertaining whether there has been or is a contravention of the Act. For the same reason the restriction on the Inspector's powers noted in para 9.45 apply to this power. If the records are maintained by the retailer on computer the Inspector may require the records to be produced in a form in which they may be taken away.

9.47 To enable him to deal specifically with issues relating to the size of shops, the Inspector is given powers to take measurements and photographs for the purposes of ascertaining whether there has been a contravention or is a contravention of the Act. In support of these extensive powers an offence of obstructing an Inspector is created by Sch 2, para 4 (see Chapter 10).

The Jewish exemption

9.48 The local authority is given powers under Sch 2, Part II of the 1994 Act to deal with contraventions of the Jewish exemption. By para 8(11) a local authority may cancel a notice giving the exemption where a person has been convicted of an offence under para 8(10). For a fuller description of these powers, see Chapter 8.

Loading control areas

9.49 As has been described in Chapter 6, under Sch 3 the local authority has the power—
    (a) to resolve that its area shall become a loading control area;
    (b) to attach conditions to the grant of a consent to a retailer;
    (c) to ensure that the applicant for a consent pays a reasonable fee; and
    (d) to revoke consents or amend the conditions attached to them in the event of an offence being committed in their area by the retailer concerned.

10 The offences and defences

INTRODUCTION

10.1 In this Chapter the offences created by the Sunday Trading Act 1994 are examined in detail and the penalties created for each offence are set out and discussed. Similarly the statutory defences are considered and analysed and the issue of the enforcement of the criminal law by use of the civil jurisdiction is considered by reference to the case law under the Shops Act 1950.

THE OFFENCES AND PENALTIES

10.2 The Sunday Trading Act 1994 creates five separate statutory offences as follows—
(a) two relating to Sunday opening of large shops;
(b) one relating to the obstruction of Sunday trading Inspectors;
(c) one relating to the Jewish exemption; and
(d) one relating to the loading and unloading of lorries at large shops.

10.3 *The first offence relating to the opening of large shops on Sundays* is contained in the 1994 Act, Sch 1, paras 2(1), 7(1). As has been pointed out the only offence created in this respect is that contained in Sch 1, para 2(1) which imposes an absolute ban on Sunday trading by large shops except for—
(a) those which are exempted by Sch 1, para 3;
(b) those which are exempted under the Jewish exemption; and
(c) those which have given notice to the local authority of their intention to open specifying their opening hours under Sch 1, para 2(3).

10.4 Any offence therefore arising out of these provisions is an offence under Sch 1, para 7(1)—

> 'If para 2(1) above is contravened in relation to a shop, the occupier of the shop shall be liable on summary conviction to a fine not exceeding £50,000'.

10.5 The old drafting techniques for summonses will have to be retained. Summonses must allege that there is a contravention of Sch 1, para 2(1), contrary to Sch 1, para 7(1).[1]

---

[1] See *Tonkin v Raven* [1959] 1 QB 177. In this case the retailer was charged with an offence under the 1950 Act, s 50 and the Shops Regulations 1937 for failing to display a notice stating the purpose for which the shop was open on Sunday. The Magistrates dismissed the charge as showing no offence. On appeal, the Divisional Court provided that under the Act any charge had to be preferred as an offence contrary to s 47. Section 50 merely created an exception to the general rule which the defendant was required to bring himself within to avoid being convicted.

10.6 Thus, it will be for the prosecuting authority to show that the large shop was open on Sunday for the serving of retail customers. The retailer will have to show

The offences and penalties 10.13

which of the exemptions or exceptions referred to above he falls under and the burden of proving this will fall upon him.[1] Just as under the 1950 Act therefore, only one offence is created for opening a shop on Sunday.[2]

---

[1] See the Magistrates' Courts Act 1980, s 101.
[2] *B & Q (Retail) Ltd v Dudley Metropolitan Borough Council* (1987) 86 LGR 137.

10.7 *The second offence relating to the opening of large shops on Sundays* is contained in the 1994 Act, Sch 1, para 7(2). This offence relates to the duty of a retailer under para 6 to exhibit a notice specifying the permitted Sunday opening hours which must be displayed in a conspicuous position inside and outside the shop. In the case of a breach of that duty, para 7(2) provides that the occupier of a shop shall be liable on summary conviction to a fine not exceeding level 2 on the standard scale. The maximum fine under level 2 is currently £500.

10.8 The local authority must show that a large shop was open on Sunday for the serving of retail customers and that it was only open due to the fact that the general ban on Sunday trading was excluded because notice had been served on the local authority showing the permitted opening hours of that shop. The prosecuting authority will then have to show that no notice has been displayed in a conspicuous position either inside or outside the shop or both, or that it contains inaccurate information.

10.9 *The third offence created by the 1994 Act is that relating to Sunday trading Inspectors*, contained in Sch 2, para 4.

10.10 This provision provides—

'Any person who intentionally obstructs an Inspector appointed under para 3 above acting in the execution of his duty shall be liable on summary conviction to a fine not exceeding level 3 on the standard scale.'

The maximum fine under level 3 is currently £1,000.

10.11 *The fourth offence created by the 1994 Act is that contained in Sch 2, para 8(10)*. This offence relates to the Jewish exemption, as to which see Chapter 8.

10.12 Sch 2, para 8(10) provides—

'A person who, in a notice or certificate given for the purposes of this paragraph, makes a statement which is false in a material respect and which he knows to be false or does not believe to be true shall be liable on summary conviction to a fine not exceeding level 5 on the standard scale'.

The maximum fine under level 5 is currently £5,000.

10.13 The prosecution must therefore show that the notice given in this case by the occupier was false in that the person concerned is not a person of the Jewish religion and/or that he did not intend to keep the shop concerned closed for the serving of customers on the Jewish Sabbath. Similarly any certificate given by a Minister of the Synagogue or the Secretary of the Synagogue or a nominated person that the person concerned is a person of the Jewish religion, which is false, may also be the subject of prosecution.

10.14 *The offences and defences*

10.14 The prosecution have to show that the person who it is alleged has committed the offence 'knows (the statement) to be false or does not believe (it) to be true'. It is to be noted however, that the opening of a shop on the Jewish Sabbath does not constitute an offence although clearly it may be evidence of the falsity of the notice or certificate which has been given.

10.15 *The final offence created by the 1994 Act is that contained in Sch 3, para 9.* This offence is in the following terms—

'A person who contravenes paragraph 2 above shall be liable on summary conviction to a fine not exceeding level 3 on the standard scale'.

The maximum fine under level 3 is currently £1,000.

10.16 Schedule 3, para 2 forbids the loading or unloading of goods from a vehicle at a large shop situated in a loading control area without the consent of the local authority or in breach of any conditions subject to which such consent is granted.

10.17 Hence it is for the prosecution to show—
(a) that the area in question is designated a loading control area;
(b) that the shop at which the loading or unloading occurs is a large shop within the meaning of Sch 1 to the 1994 Act and in respect of which a notice under Sch 1, para 4 has effect.
(c) that goods were being loaded or unloaded from a vehicle at that shop before 9.00am.
(d) that such loading or unloading is in connection with the trade or business carried on in that shop.

Prosecution of directors

10.18 Schedule 2, para 6(1) provides that where an offence has been committed by a body corporate and it is proved that it has been committed with the consent or connivance of or is due to the negligence of any director, manager, secretary or other similar officer or a person who indeed is purporting to act in such capacity, that person as well as the company shall be guilty of an offence. Thus there is now clear statutory authority that officers of companies can be guilty of an offence provided that the offence itself has first been committed by the body corporate. This express statutory provision may well overcome the difficulties which prosecuting authorities have experienced in the past in seeking to enforce the 1950 Act against directors and officers of the company.

10.19 By para 6(2) if companies are managed by their members then the acts and defaults of members in connection with their functions of management will be treated as if they had been committed or neglected by the member as if by a director of the company. These provisions are in a new and different form the provisions of the 1950 Act, s 71(5), (6).

10.20 Coupled with the powers to seize records etc given elsewhere in the 1994 Act, the prosecution should be able to prove that some or all members of senior management were aware of the breach of the Act and can thus be prosecuted.

10.21 Section 71(5) of the 1950 Act[1] gave rise to a number of issues. The first issue was whether a store manager was 'a Manager' within the meaning of the section. The

The offences and penalties 10.25

same issue arises by virtue of Sch 2, para 6(1). In *Tesco Supermarkets Ltd v Nattrass*[2] the word 'manager' in relation to a similar piece of legislation was given a restricted interpretation, namely someone who was in a position of managing the affairs of the company itself.

[1] This section provided 'Where an offence for which the occupier of a shop is liable under this Act has, in fact, been committed by some manager, agent, servant or other person, the manager, servant or other person shall be liable to the like penalty as if he were the occupier'.
[2] *Tesco Supermarkets Ltd v Nattrass* [1972] AC 153.

10.22 In the *Tesco* case the provision with which the courts were concerned was the Trade Descriptions Act 1968, s 20(1)[1]. That section, as is apparent from the footnote, is very similar to that now contained in Sch 2, para 6(1) of the 1994 Act. It appears therefore that a store manager could not be convicted of an offence under para 6(1) whereas he might well have been under s 71(5) of the 1950 Act.

[1] This section provides 'Where an offence under this Act which has been committed by a body corporate is proved to have been committed with the consent and connivance of, or to be attributable to any neglect on the part of, any director, manager, secretary or other similar officer of the body corporate, or any person who was purporting to act in any such capacity, he as well as the body corporate shall be guilty of that offence . . . .'

10.23 Secondly if the occupier had been successfully prosecuted and had not sought to blame any other person under the 1950 Act, s 71(6), was it open to the prosecution to seek to prosecute any other persons under s 71(5)? That issue appears never to have been the subject of any authoritative decision, but has, however, been resolved by the wording of Sch 2, para 6(1), clearly showing that any such person 'as well' as the company will be capable of being convicted.

10.24 There has been some history in the past of directors and other officers of retailers being prosecuted by the local authorities pursuant to the Magistrates' Courts Act 1980, s 44[1]. It became clear that due to the apparent overlap between s 71(5) of the 1950 Act and s 44 of the 1980 Act it could be argued that s 44 had no application at all.

[1] This section provides that 'A person who aids, abets, counsels or procures the commission by another person of a summary offence shall be guilty of the like offence . . . .'

10.25 By virtue of the Interpretation Act 1978, s 18, which is headed 'duplicate offences',[1] it was thought unlikely that the mere fact of the overlap would indicate a contrary intention under the Interpretation Act. However, it was argued that s 71(5) was substitutionary in nature, ie that the servant, manager or agent was not intended to be an additional victim but to be prosecuted only in substitution for the occupier. If this was so there would be a fundamental conflict and difference between the liability of a manager under the 1950 Act and under the 1980 Act. Hence it could be said there was a contrary intention.

[1] Section 18 provides—
'Where an act or omission constitutes an offence under two or more Acts, or both under an Act and at common law, the offender shall, unless the contrary intention appears, be liable to be prosecuted and punished under either or any of those Acts or at common law, but shall not be liable to be punished for more than once for the same offence'.

10.26 *The offences and defences*

10.26 It appears unlikely, given the clear statutory authority to prosecute directors and officers of the company under the 1994 Act, Sch 2, para 6 that these issues are going to be of relevance to enforcement authorities and/or directors and officers of retailers after the commencement of the 1994 Act.

'Occupiers'

10.27 As it can be seen, three of the five statutory offences can only be committed by the 'occupier'. Who then is an occupier under the 1994 Act? Under the 1950 Act it was also the occupier who was the person to be prosecuted. There is little case law on who is or is not the occupier for the purposes of the 1950 Act.

10.28 It is clear that a company may be an occupier.[1] The lack of clarity in the expression however is illustrated when considering the position of licensed premises where it has been held that the brewers who had put in a manager as licensee could be the occupiers.[2]

---

[1] *Evans and Co Ltd v LCC* [1914] 3 KB 315.
[2] *Liverpool Corporation v Peter Walker and Son Ltd* (1913) 77 JP Jo 402.

10.29 Enforcement authorities usually will be protected by either the Companies Act 1985, s 348 or the provisions of the Business Names Act 1985, ss 1, 4(1)(b) from choosing the wrong person as an occupier. The first provision under the Companies Act requires every company to paint or affix its name on the outside of any place in which its business is carried on. The Business Names Act 1985, s 4(1)(b) imposes an obligation on the person to whom the Act applies, to ensure that in any premises where the business is carried on and to which customers have access, to display in a prominent position a notice containing the name and addresses of the owners of the business so that it may be easily read by customers or suppliers.

10.30 Many local authorities have in the past failed to prosecute the correct occupier under the 1950 Act with the effect that summonses which have been issued against the wrongly named occupier have been dismissed.

Penalties

10.31 The fine of £50,000 for the main offence created by the Act has been criticised as being disproportionate. It has been suggested that the penalty should be proportionate to those imposed by statute for activities of comparable gravity. In general, it is argued that it is a reasonable inference that the level of maximum fine identified by Parliament should be proportionate to the 'social evil' perceived; and Parliament should seek to maintain a balance, in setting a maximum fine, between the 'social evils'. In contemplating a maximum fine of £50,000 the legislator must contemplate the imposition of a fine 10 times as great as the identical conduct committed on Sundays under the 1950 Act. It is rare for magistrates to have the power to impose a fine greater than £5,000, and even then the occasions when they do so are often those when the offence is of the kind where imprisonment is an alternative.

10.32 In defence of Parliament however, it must be said that the widespread flouting of the law, not only by major retailers but as a matter of course over many decades by small shops, and the resulting need for local authorities to have recourse to

Enforcement 10.37

the civil courts to secure observance of the 1950 Act, was sufficient reason for Parliament to legislate for such penalty so that in future the same lack of respect for the criminal law would not be seen. It will be interesting to monitor the level of fines imposed by the courts for any breaches of the new law should any occur, certainly in cases where the breaches are both flagrant and continuous.

Offences due to the fault of another person

10.33   Schedule 2, para 5 of the 1994 Act allows the prosecuting authority to proceed not only against the occupier of the shop whom it alleges has committed the offence but also against some other person either instead of or as well as that occupier. It reads—

> 'Where the commission by any person of an offence under this Act is due to the act or default of some other person, that other person shall be guilty of the offence, and a person may be charged with and convicted of the offence by virtue of this paragraph whether or not proceedings are taken against the first mentioned person'.

10.34   Thus if the prosecution can show for instance that the store in question was open outside the six hour period due entirely to the negligence of or the deliberate act of the store manager then that local authority may decide to prosecute the store manager as well as the occupier, or alternatively may decide to prosecute him instead of the retailer. This provision coupled with the defence of due diligence enables the court to ensure that the appropriate person responsible for the commission of the offence is convicted.

ENFORCEMENT

Magistrates' court

10.35   The 1950 Act gave jurisdiction only to the magistrates' court to determine whether or not there was a breach of that Act (and courts on appeal therefrom). The 1994 Act gives the same jurisdiction, by Sch 1, para 7(1), (2), which provides that if an offence has been committed under the Act, the occupier will be liable on summary conviction to a fine.

Who may prosecute?

10.36   The local authority has a duty to enforce the 1994 Act. The issue arises however, as to whether it is only the local authority who can enforce or whether a private citizen can take out proceedings himself in the local magistrates' court. This issue is one which had not previously been decided under the 1950 Act or the 1936 Act until July 1994.

10.37   The matter was the subject of a judgment of the Divisional Court on 14 July 1994[1] in a judicial review in which Tescos, Superdrug and Woolworths sought a judicial review of the decision of the Harrow magistrates' court to allow Mr Roy Edey (an inveterate campaigner against Sunday trading) to issue summonses alleging breaches of s 47 of the 1950 Act.

10.37 *The offences and defences*

---

[1] *R v Harrow Justices ex p Woolworths plc,* Divisional Court Butler-Sloss LJ and MacPhearson J, CO/322/94, unreported judgment 14 July 1994.

10.38 The issues were as follows—
(a) where an information is laid by a person who is not entitled to prosecute, the information is a nullity and the Court cannot try it or convict on it;[1]
(b) in general however, where an offence is alleged to have been committed, a private individual may always commence a prosecution. This right is in order to safeguard against inertia or worse, by a law enforcement agency;[2]
(c) there are exceptions to this general principle; namely in cases where there are no private prosecutions at all or the right to prosecute privately is subject to partial restrictions.[3] In other cases prosecution can only be taken out by an individual with the consent of the Attorney General;
(d) the question is whether or not the 1994 Act (or indeed the 1950 Act) reserve the right to prosecute a specified person or persons only, namely the local authority.

---

[1] *Oberst v Coombs* (1955) 53 LGR 316.
[2] *Gouriet v Union of Post Office Workers* [1978] AC 435.
[3] See for instance, the Weights and Measures Act 1985, s 83.

10.39 It is clear, however, that in 'Shops Act' cases a local authority's solicitor could prosecute, even though s 71(2) of the 1950 Act provided for the appointment by the local authority of Inspectors and empowered the Inspectors to prosecute.[1] The question did not arise in that case however of whether a private prosecution could be undertaken.

---

[1] See *Kirklees MBC v Wickes Building Supplies Ltd* (1983) 82 LGR 467.

10.40 There were some obiter statements in *R v Norwich Justices ex p Texas Homecare Ltd*[1] which supported the view that only local authorities could prosecute under the 1950 Act.

---

[1] (1991) CO/1895/89, Crim LR 555.

10.41 In the case referred to in para 10.37 it was suggested that due to the previous structure of legislation consolidated into the 1950 Act, it was not an Act which an individual, rather than the local authority, was entitled to enforce. The court however, held that the 1950 Act could be enforced by private prosecution. The same may not be true of the 1994 Act. However the decision of the court is a powerful indicator that the 1994 Act may be enforced by individuals, although it is not necessarily conclusive.

Injunctions

10.42 The use of the civil jurisdiction to obtain injunctions to restrain breaches of the criminal law has been used most frequently in the field of Sunday trading.

Enforcement 10.48

10.43   In this section therefore the powers of the local authority to seek injunctions to restrain breaches of the 1994 Act are reviewed with reference to the previous case law in connection with the enforcement of the 1950 Act. Consideration is given to the material differences between the two Acts and how these might affect both the ability of local authorities to seek injunctions and the effect it should have on the way these actions are conducted. The jurisdiction of civil courts in such cases is an exceptional jurisdiction 'in support of the criminal law'.[1]

[1]   *Gouriet v Union of Post Office Workers* [1978] AC 435.

10.44   The jurisdiction to seek an injunction from the civil courts to prevent an anticipated breach of the criminal law is also an exceptional one, and should be exercised with 'the greatest delicacy and caution':[1] 'Something more than infringement of the criminal law must be shown before it is proper for a local authority to seek and the court to grant an injunction'.[2]

[1]   *Gouriet v Union of Post Office Workers* [1978] AC 435.
[2]   *Stoke-on-Trent City Council v B & Q (Retail) Ltd* [1984] 1 AC 754.

10.45   Save in exceptional cases, the court should not give a declaratory judgment, ruling on whether certain conduct alleged to be criminal is or is not unlawful, but should stay civil proceedings in favour of allowing the matter to be resolved in the criminal courts.[1]

[1]   *Imperial Tobacco Ltd and Another v Attorney General* [1981] AC 718.

10.46   The power of a local authority to obtain a final injunction in support of the criminal law is based upon the Local Government Act 1972, s 222.[1]

[1]   This section provides—
    'Where a local authority consider it expedient for the promotion or protection of the interests of the inhabitants of their area—
    (a)   they may prosecute or defend or appear in any legal proceedings and, in the case of civil proceedings, may institute them in their own name, . . .'

10.47   By virtue of s 222 together with the duty to enforce contained in the 1950 Act, s 47 allowed a local authority to seek injunctions to restrain breaches of s 47. The House of Lords in *Stoke v B & Q*[1] resisted a determined attack on the existence of this power by B & Q.

[1]   *Stoke-on-Trent City Council v B & Q (Retail) Ltd* [1984] 1 AC 754.

10.48   Similarly the House of Lords in *Kirklees v Wickes*[1] made it clear that, in view of the specific wording of the 1950 Act, s 71(1) ('to secure observance') a statutory duty was imposed on a local authority to take civil proceedings for an injunction if they were necessary.

[1]   *Kirklees MBC v Wickes Building Supplies Ltd* [1993] AC 227.

10.49 *The offences and defences*

10.49 What then should a local authority, before passing a Resolution under s 222, consider before deciding how to proceed to enforce the 1994 Act?

10.50 It has been powerfully submitted that local authorities should be acting in accordance with the principles which previously guided the Attorney General in his use of the civil jurisdiction to enforce the criminal law.[1]

---

1   See for instance, *Stoke-on-Trent City Council v B & Q (Retail) Ltd* [1984] CH1 at 26 C - H per Ackner LJ 32 D - E and 26G to 33A Oliver LJ and [1984] AC 754 at 776C, per Lord Templeman.

10.51 The effect of s 222 means that local authorities could proceed in their own name without proceeding under the relator procedure. Under the latter procedure the decision to bring civil proceedings is the Attorney General's alone and cannot be delegated.

10.52 Under the 1994 Act it is submitted that it is a proper practice for local authorities first of all to seek to prosecute the alleged offender to see whether they can establish a breach of the criminal law. If they have established a breach of the criminal law and the retailer continues to trade in breach of the appropriate terms of the 1994 Act then the local authority should consider that further prosecutions may result in substantial fines, bearing in mind the new fine limit of £50,000 contained in the Act. In those circumstances a series of penalties of a substantial sum is likely to have the effect of ensuring that a retailer complies with the 1994 Act.

10.53 In view of the level of the fine it is thought highly unlikely that a civil court would be prepared to grant an injunction under the new Act unless there had been first a recourse to the criminal law. Where local authorities do proceed, the *Wickes* case is clear authority for the proposition that, if it is suggested that the defendant has a defence, the point should be tested immediately either by treating the hearing of the motion for interlocutory relief as the trial of the action itself, or by some other means such as Order 14[1] proceedings. This appears to be the case even though (perhaps especially so) if the defence raised is one under EC law and results in a reference to the European Court under Article 177 of the EC Treaty.

---

1   Rules of the Supreme Court 1965, SI 1965/1776, Order 14.

10.54 It also appears possible that such applications for injunctions can be brought in the county court pursuant to the County Courts Act 1984, s 22. That section gives the county court jurisdiction in respect of or relating to any land or the use or enjoyment of any land. The question is whether the trading on Sunday in a large shop comes within the ordinary meaning of the section and of course whether the land in question falls within the rateable value limits of the county court.[1]

---

1   See *Newport Borough Council v Khan (Sabz Ali) and Others* [1990] 1 WLR 1185.

10.55 The final issue which arises on the local authorities' rights to obtain injunctions to support the criminal law is the question of whether or not such a local authority is required as a matter of law to offer a cross undertaking as to damage. This issue also was resolved by the House of Lords in the *Kirklees* and *Wickes* case.

10.56   In the *Hoffmann-LaRoche* case[1] it was decided that the Crown was not required to give an undertaking for damages when it was involved in law enforcement and in particular where the statute in question provided expressly for enforcement by civil proceedings.

[1]   F *Hoffmann-La Roche & Co AG and Others v Secretary of State for Trade and Industry* [1975] AC 295.

10.57   The position in a relator action was different. Once the Attorney General's consent had been obtained the relator stood in the position of a plaintiff in an ordinary suit between subject and subject and an undertaking in damages was required from the relator but not from the Attorney General.

10.58   In the *Wickes* and *Kirklees* case in the first instance[1] Mr Justice Mervyn Davies decided that it was a matter of discretion as to whether or not he would require such a cross undertaking and declined to demand one from the prosecuting authority.

[1]   *Kirklees MBC v Wickes Building Supplies Ltd* [1990] 1 WLR 1237.

10.59   In the Court of Appeal case[1] the Court concluded that the discretionary power not to require an undertaking in damages in a law enforcement action was 'a privilege for the Crown alone' and discharged injunctions granted against both B & Q and *Wickes* following the refusal of the local authorities to offer such a cross undertaking.

[1]   *Kirklees MBC v Wickes Building Supplies Ltd* [1991] 3 CMLR 282, CA.

10.60   The House of Lords,[1] having extensively considered both the English and the EC issues involved in the Appeal, concluded that it was an issue of discretion as to whether or not a cross undertaking should be exacted in these cases. In 'Shops Act' cases the judge should take into account whether or not the retailer would, unless restrained, continue to act in contravention of the Act. He should take into account if he is aware of it, the effect of requiring an undertaking and in particular whether it had caused the collapse of law enforcement in this area of law, and he was entitled to take into account the effect that breaches of the law might have on other retailers.

[1]   *Kirklees MBC v Wickes Building Supplies Ltd* [1992] 3 WLR 171, HL.

10.61   In conclusion therefore it appears that a local authority seeking to enforce the 1994 Act, having satisfied itself that the use of the criminal law even with its high penalties will not ensure compliance, may have recourse to the civil courts to do so. Whether or not an injunction will be granted to assist that local authority will depend on the particular facts of the matter and how the Court dealing with the matter decides to deal with any issue of discretion involved. It appears that in the usual case it will be unlikely that the court will require an authority to offer a cross undertaking in damages, but in certain circumstances, especially if the court forms a view that there is a strong defence to any action, it may find itself compelled to do so.

10.62 *The offences and defences*

DEFENCES

10.62 In this section of the Chapter the statutory defences created by the 1994 Act are examined and consideration is given to general defences and in particular those which have been before the European Court or which are currently outstanding.

Shopping up time

10.63 The 1994 Act, Sch 1, para 8 provides a defence to the offence of having a large store open for the serving of customers on Sundays outside the six-hour period. The defence is in the following terms—

> 'Where a person is charged with having contravened paragraph 2(1) above, in relation to a large shop which was permitted to be open for the serving of retail customers on the Sunday in question during the permitted Sunday opening hours specified in a notice under paragraph 4 above, by reason of his having served a retail customer after the end of those hours, it shall be a defence to prove that the customer was in the shop before that time and left not later than half an hour after that time'.

This defence is very similar in terms to ss 1(7), 2(3), 56(3) of the 1950 Act,[1] and thus guidance may be had from the decisions of the courts in connection with this type of defence as it exists under the 1950 Act.[2]

---

[1] Section 1(7) 'Early Closing days' states—
'Nothing in this section shall prevent the serving of a customer at any time at which the shop is required to be closed under this section if it is proved either that the customer was in the shop before the time when the shop was required to be closed, or that there was reasonable ground for believing that the article supplied to the customer was required in the case of illness.'
Section 2(3) 'General closing hours' states—
'Nothing in this section shall prevent—
  (a) the serving of a customer where it is proved that the customer was in the shop before the closing hour, or that reasonable grounds existed for believing that the article supplied after the closing hour to a customer was required in the case of illness; or
  (b) any transaction mentioned in the Second Schedule to this Act.'
Section 56(3) 'Sunday trading' states—
'Where any person is charged with keeping open for the serving of customers in contravention of this Part of this Act a shop which is permitted to be open until a certain hour by reason of his having served a customer after that hour, it shall be a good defence that the customer was in the shop before that hour and left the shop not later than half-an-hour after that hour.'

[2] *Salford Cattle Market Salerooms Ltd v Osborne* [1923] All ER Rep 312 (in which it was held that this defence does not apply if customers are specifically invited into the store immediately before closing time with a view to serving them afterwards) and *Moore v Tweedale* [1935] 2 KB 163 (in which it was held that it was perfectly acceptable for a hairdresser who had a customer in before closing time knowing that the treatment of that customer would go on past the statutory closing time).

The defence of due diligence

10.64 Schedule 2, para 7 of the 1994 Act sets out in a modern form a defence of due diligence. This defence applies to all of the five offences created by the Act. It reflects the due diligence defence previously contained in the 1950 Act, s 71(6).[1] The wording of para 7(1) is similar to the Consumer Protection Act 1987, s 24.

Defences 10.68

---

[1] Section 71(6) states—
'Where the occupier of a shop is charged with an offence under this Act, he shall be entitled upon information duly laid by him to have any other person whom he charges as the actual offender brought before the court at the time appointed for hearing the charge; and if, after the commission of the offence has been proved, he proves to the satisfaction of the court that he has used due diligence to enforce the execution of this Act and that the said other person has committed the offence in question without his knowledge, consent or connivance, the said other person shall be summarily convicted of such offence, and the occupier shall be exempt from any fine.'

10.65 How will such a defence be used in the area of Sunday trading? There appears to be no reported case of any decisions under the 1950 Act, s 71(6). This may perhaps be surprising bearing in mind the fact that most shops were entitled to open under the Act provided they only sold products which fell within the Fifth Schedule of the Act. One might have anticipated the use of the defence in situations where retailers were genuinely trying to comply with the Fifth Schedule but which for some reason, perhaps due to inefficiency of their staff, sales were taking place of products which should not have been sold.

10.66 What then are the likely areas in which the defence may be of use under the 1994 Act? First in connection with the main offence it seems that there must be in place clear systems to ensure—

(a) that any premises which are not a 'shop' are monitored to ensure that they do not become a 'shop'. Thus for instance a video hire shop which also sells videos must have a system in place to ensure that its turnover, transaction numbers and other similar details are noted and reviewed periodically, to ensure that it continues to pass the 'wholly or mainly' test, if it is to have a defence under the Act. If it has such a system and for one week the test was infringed it appears that the occupier might well have a defence;

(b) that for any shops that open pursuant to the provisions relating to permitted opening hours the defence may be of use. Here the system must address the following issues—

   (i) the service of the notice on the local authority;
   (ii) that the store opens and closes on time;
   (iii) the shopping up provisions;
   (iv) the preventing of serving of customers outside the six-hour period especially if the store stays open thereafter for lawful purposes, eg if it is a pharmacy or a hire shop.

10.67 As regards the display of the statutory notices, the fact that the notice is destroyed by vandals or blows down in a gale or is removed by a junior member of staff without authority, may be circumstances where if the appropriate systems are in force, a defence may succeed.

10.68 As has previously been explained the offences created by this Act, save as otherwise noted, create absolute prohibitions. They are thus 'absolute offences'. It is irrelevant that the defendant did not intend to break the law. All that has to be shown is clear evidence that the Act in question has been contravened. That is all that is required for a conviction to become inevitable. For this reason the defence of due diligence is essential to have some degree of fairness.

10.69   *The offences and defences*

10.69   However, there must be some positive action by a retailer under the 1994 Act if the retailer hopes successfully to rely on the defence. He cannot simply sit back and do nothing and then expect to convince a Court that he has acted reasonably in connection with the matter. In connection with large retailers, there is important case law as to whether they can use the defence to be able to rely on acts or omissions of its employees.

10.70   Thus in *Tesco Supermarkets Ltd v Nattrass*,[1] the House of Lords upheld an appeal by Tescos enabling them to rely on the act or omission of a shop manager in failing to supervise a young employee arranging packets of washing powder marked with a higher price than that for which they were actually for sale.

[1]   *Tesco Supermarkets Ltd v Nattrass* [1972] AC 153.

10.71   There are a number of useful cases showing the sort of steps which is it anticipated that retailers and others should take to successfully employ the defence. Although each case usually depends on its own facts, it is possible to set a standard of tests the Courts will usually apply.[1]

[1]   See for instance, *Baxters (Butchers) v Manley* (1985) 4 Tr L 219 and *Bibby-Cheshire v Golden Wonder* [1972] 1 WLR 1487.

10.72   In practice therefore it can probably be said that it must be possible for the retailer in question under the 1994 Act to demonstrate that senior management are aware of the major provisions of the Act, that there is a proper system to ensure that the relevant members of management both at store or head office level are aware of the steps which need to be taken to ensure proper compliance with the law and that there must be adequate systems in place to ensure adequate supervision at all levels of the company. Also proper training must have been given as to the statutory requirements and there must be a proper system in place to monitor the systems to ensure compliance.

10.73   Schedule 2, para 7(2) of the 1994 Act, in common with similar provisions in respect of consumer protection law, deals with the situation where a retailer wishes to use the defence that the commission of the offence that they have been charged with was due to the act or default of another person. In order to rely on this defence it must, at least seven clear days before the hearing, serve on the prosecutor a notice in writing identifying or assisting the identification of the person who in fact committed the offence. If the defence fails to comply with this procedure it may not be entitled to rely on that defence without the leave of the Court. Faced with that defence the prosecution may make use of Sch 2, para 5 and prosecute that other person either with the retailer involved or instead of him.

The European defences

10.74   The 1950 Act has been the subject of repeated attacks in the last few years in the courts as being contrary to various provisions of EC law. Basically these attacks are in two areas, the first in respect of Article 30 of the EC Treaty and the second a current challenge that the law was contrary to the Equal Treatment Directive[1] and the Sex Discrimination Act 1975.

[1] 76/207/EEC, OJ No L39, 14.2.76, p 40.

10.75 The Article 30 issue, so far as the courts in England and Wales are concerned, has finally been resolved by the decision of the European Court in the *Stoke* and *Norwich* cases.[1]

[1] *Stoke on Trent City Council v B & Q plc.* Case C-169–91 [1993] 1 All ER 481.

10.76 Also the use of Article 30 to defend criminal proceedings before the national courts on the basis that the national measure in question is inconsistent with Article 30 of the EC Treaty appears to have been substantially curtailed by the landmark decision of the European Court in *Keck*.[1]

[1] *B Keck and D Mithoud.* Joined Cases C/262/91 and C/268/91 ECJ.

10.77 The other main challenge to the 1950 Act relying on European law is the challenge of B & Q and a number of its shopworkers that the provisions of the 1950 Act discriminated against female shopworkers and were hence contrary both to the Sex Discrimination Act 1975 and to the Equal Treatment Directive.[1] This case has been the subject of a decision of the High Court.[2]

[1] 76/207/EEC, OJ No L39, 14.2.76, p 40.
[2] *Chisholm and Others v Kirklees Metropolitan Borough Council and Her Majesty's Attorney General* and *Kirklees Metropolitan Borough Council v B & Q plc* (1993) unreported judgment of Ferris J, 26 May 1993.

10.78 By reason of the European Court's decision in *Keck* it appears that the 1994 Act which considerably liberalises Sunday trading will not be the subject of any further challenge under Article 30 unless (in the very unlikely situation) there was any evidence that imported goods were in some way being disadvantaged compared with home produced goods.

10.79 Similarly it appears that because of the increased employment opportunities which will arise for female part time shopworkers as a result of the 1994 Act it will be unlikely that any challenge will or could be mounted to the 1994 Act based on the Equal Treatment Directive argument.

11 Shop worker protection

INTRODUCTION

11.1 Throughout the debate about which of the options to reform the Sunday trading laws should be chosen, one common feature ran through all of the campaigning bodies' proposals, namely the question of adequate protection for shop workers. The nature and extent of that protection in the proposals varied but the main campaigning organisations favoured three basic protections—
    (a) protection to ensure that Sunday work was entirely voluntary;
    (b) the retention of premium pay for Sunday work; and
    (c) time off in lieu of Sunday work.

11.2 In addition the SHRC proposed that there should be a limitation on the maximum number of hours that an employee could be required to work in the retail trade.

11.3 From the outset the Government indicated that it was prepared to legislate to ensure that Sunday work in the retail sector was indeed voluntary on Sundays. As explained in Chapter 1 the Government imposed a three line whip in respect of all of the employment provisions in the Bill. Those provisions were substantially altered and strengthened by consent during the progress of the Bill. Attempts however to legislate for premium pay, maximum hours of work on Sundays, and pre-entry discrimination were all rejected by both Houses.

11.4 Nevertheless, the 1994 Act will give substantial protection to shop workers. It will impose new obligations on employers, including those who currently lawfully trade on Sundays. The extent of the protection is widespread in that it affects a large class of people who work in or about shops. In addition, not only is there a very wide definition of people who are to be protected but also a wide definition of what constitutes a shop. Thus, not only those premises which are covered by the trading provisions of the Act as shops but also many other types of premises are included in the definition for these purposes.

WHO IS PROTECTED?

11.5 The employment protection measures of the 1994 Act are contained in s 4 and Sch 4. Schedule 4 contains a number of key definitions in para 1.

11.6 *Who is a shop worker?* A 'shop worker' is defined as meaning—
    'An employee who, under his contract of employment, is required to do shop work or may be required to do such work'.

11.7 'Shop work' itself is defined as meaning—
    'Work in or about a shop in England or Wales on a day on which the shop is open for the serving of customers'.

11.8 It is therefore apparent that the protection is only extended to those who work in England and Wales.

11.9 It is clear that the class of person who is protected is very wide. It covers all store management staff; those who work in warehouses attached to stores, and depending on the facts it may well cover employees who are delivery drivers attached to a specific store, and even cleaning or maintenance staff who work in or about a shop.

11.10 However, it is clear from the definition that the protection does not extend to staff who work in the Head Office of a retail company, nor to those who work in distribution centres, nor to delivery drivers whose job it is to deliver goods to the store on a Sunday, and it is unlikely to protect area or regional management.

11.11 The issue of 'who is a shop worker?' is one of fact which will have to be determined by the Industrial Tribunal in each case. It should be noted that there are three key elements—
    (a) the worker must work in or about a shop;
    (b) he must do that work on a day on which the shop is open for the serving of customers; and
    (c) he must be required under his contract of employment to do such work.

11.12 As is apparent from the two key definitions set out in paras 11.6 and 11.7, protection is only given to those who work in a 'shop'. What then for these purposes is a 'shop' under the Act? Here there are two key definitions and some explanatory paragraphs of the definition section to be considered.

11.13 A 'shop' is defined as including—

'any premises where any retail trade or business is carried on'.

As fully explained in Chapter 2, this definition is in effect the same as that contained in the 1950 Act and all of the commentary on the 1950 Act provisions are therefore applicable to the issue so far as it affects employment protection measures in the Act.

11.14 The question of what is a 'retail trade or business'? has also been addressed at length in Chapter 2. For these purposes Sch 4, para 1 defines 'retail trade or business' as including—

'(a) the business of a barber or hairdresser,
(b) the business of hiring goods otherwise than for use in the course of a trade or business, and
(c) retail sales by auction'.

11.15 From this definition it appears clear therefore that irrespective of the outcome of the current litigation as to whether video hire shops are shops under the 1950 Act (as to which see Chapter 2) those working in hairdresser shops, video or plant hire shops, and auctioneers and their staff working in auction rooms are all employed in a retail trade or business. It may be, subject to the outcome of the litigation to which reference has been made, that those who work in other service industries repairing goods or cleaning may also have the benefit of the protection given by this section. It appears unlikely however that estate agents or travel agents will have this protection, by reason of the case law under the 1950 Act.

11.16 The 1994 Act specifically deals with certain businesses which would otherwise be retail businesses by excluding from protection those who work in catering businesses or those who work at theatres and places of amusements selling programmes, catalogues and similar items. These exclusions are achieved by including in the definition of 'retail trade or business' the following—

'but [retail trade or business] does not include catering business or the sale at theatres and places of amusement of programmes, catalogues and similar items'.

11.17   The 1994 Act also contains a definition of what is a 'catering business'. This is defined as meaning—

'(a)   the sale of meals, refreshments or intoxicating liquor[1] for consumption on the premises on which they are sold, or

(b)   the sales of meals or refreshments prepared to order for immediate consumption off the premises'.

---
1   See para 5.6.

11.18   Thus it can be seen that employees working in hotels, public houses, cafés and restaurants and wine bars and other similar establishments will not be given the protection given to other shop workers. Neither will those who work in take-away food shops, or those who work only in restaurants within stores.

11.19   Leaving aside the policy reasons for this exclusion, it was necessary bearing in mind the case law under the 1950 Act to have a specific exclusion otherwise 'shop workers' would have included those who worked in these establishments. However, those who work in off licences are not involved in a catering business as defined and will have the benefit of the protection.

11.20   Schedule 4, para 1(2) deals with such premises as cash-and-carries, retail clubs, and the wholesale traders. These provisions may in practice be difficult to apply. The sub-paragraph reads as follows—

'Where premises are used mainly for purposes other than those of retail trade or business and would not apart from sub-paragraph (1) above be regarded as a shop, only such part of the premises as—
 (a)   is used wholly or mainly[1] for the purposes of retail trade or business, or
 (b)   is used both for the purposes of retail trade or business and for the purposes of wholesale trade and is used wholly or mainly for those two purposes considered together,
is to be regarded as a shop for the purposes of this Schedule'.

---
1   See paras 2.34–2.40.

11.21   It appears for instance that a large gift shop either in a church, museum, art gallery or other similar establishment may well be caught by the provisions contained in Sch 4, para 1(2)(a) in that the premises taken as a whole are not usually described as 'a shop' but the employee who works in that portion of the premises which constitutes 'the shop' will be protected as being a 'shop worker' under the Act. However, those who work elsewhere in the building will not be so protected.

11.22   As to those who work in cash-and-carries, wholesale warehouses, and retail clubs, they will have the protection as if they were working solely in a retail trade or business. This appears apparent from Sch 4, para 1(2)(b). For these purposes para 1(3) defines 'wholesale trade' as meaning—

'the sale of goods for use or resale in the course of a business or the hire of goods for use in the course of a business'.

11.23 The other definitions contained in para 1(1) are of the greatest importance in understanding the working of the statutory protection given and will be dealt with as and when those issues are described.

THE PROTECTION GIVEN

11.24 The 1994 Act provides protection to all who work in or about shops whether they are existing shop workers at the date of the commencement of the Act or whether they commence employment after that date. The protection is given by a system which allows shop workers to opt-in and out of shop work on Sundays at will and upon giving the appropriate notices.

Protected shop workers

11.25 There are three types of shop worker who are referred to in Sch 4, namely—'protected shop workers', 'opted-out shop workers' and 'opted-in shop workers'. Protected shop workers are defined in Sch 4, para 2. In all three categories it is of course essential that the individual concerned is a shop worker in accordance with the definition explained above. For such a shop worker to become 'protected' he must comply with one of two sets of conditions.

11.26 The first set of conditions are set out in Sch 4, para 2(2) namely—
   (a) on the day before the commencement date the employee concerned was a shop worker;
   (b) he was not a Sunday only shop worker on the day before the commencement of the Act;
   (c) he was continuously employed from that date until the appropriate date (as to the meaning of 'appropriate date' see para 11.30);
   (d) throughout that period he was a shop worker (if during that period he was not governed by a contract of employment he is not required to have been a shop worker but during any part that he was governed by a contract of employment he must throughout that time have been a shop worker).

11.27 The second set of conditions are contained in Sch 4, para 2(3). There are three conditions—
   (a) that the employee concerned is a shop worker;
   (b) that his contract of employment does not and may not require him to work on Sunday; and
   (c) that the contract could not require him to work on Sundays even if the employee were to ignore the provisions of Sch 4 of the Act.

11.28 Existing shop workers therefore who are contracted to work for specific days not including Sunday and there are no contractual provisions allowing for the variation of those terms, are automatically protected shop workers upon commencement of the Act.

11.29 *Shop worker protection*

11.29 These two sets of conditions mean in effect that all shop workers who are compellable at the commencement date to work on Sundays are 'protected shop workers' by virtue of Sch 4, para 2(2) and those who are not compellable to work on Sundays are 'protected shop workers' by virtue of para 2(3).

11.30 Schedule 4, para 2(4) deals with the expression 'appropriate date'. Basically the 'appropriate date' has a very similar meaning to expressions found in the Employment Protection (Consolidation) Act 1978. Depending on the context it means either the effective date of termination of the employment, or the date of the act which constitutes a detriment to that employee, or the date on which any agreement is entered into, or the date on which a pregnant employee returns to work, or the date in relation to which the contract is to be enforced, or the end of a period in which wages or benefit are payable.

11.31 In simple terms however the effect is that a protected shop worker falling into the first set of conditions must have been continuously employed from the day before the commencement date until for instance the effective date of the termination of his contract of employment.

11.32 Similarly for the purposes of acts or defaults giving rise to detriment, the appropriate date where that act extends over a period is the first day of that period, and where in a detriment situation there is, allegedly, a deliberate failure to act by the employer, the appropriate date shall be treated as the day on which the employer decided not to do the act in question.

11.33 Where there is allegedly a deliberate failure to act, Sch 4, para 2(6) provides that in the absence of contrary evidence, the time of the employer's decision shall be either—
    (a) when he does something inconsistent with the action he should have taken; or
    (b) when the time expires within which he should reasonably have taken the action.

11.34 In certain circumstances an employee shall be treated as having satisfied either the conditions in paras 2(2)(a) or (b) on the day before the commencement date even though the employee's relationship with his employer is no longer governed by a contract of employment.

11.35 That situation arises when the day before commencement falls within a week which counts as a period of employment with the employer under the 1978 Act, Sch 13, paras 9 or 10. These provisions relate to the absence from work because of sickness, pregnancy etc and allow certain weeks to be counted as a period of employment. Similarly if the day before commencement date falls in a week which counts as a period of employment under Sch 13, para 20, the shop worker shall be a protected one.

11.36 When dealing with the question of reinstatement or re-engagement of dismissed employees, certain weeks are allowed to be taken as counting for periods of employment in addition to falling within these provisions of the 1978 Act. The employee must also be able to show that on the last day on which his relations with his employer were governed by a contract of employment he was a shop worker and not a Sunday only shop worker.

11.37 A protected shop worker may at any time cease to be protected. This happens on the occurrence referred to in Sch 4, para 3. A protected shop worker loses his protection on or after the commencement date by giving his employer an opting-in notice. As well as giving the opting-in notice the employee must expressly agree with his employer to do shop work on Sunday or on any particular Sunday.

11.38 The 1994 Act clearly therefore envisages a two step approach to opting-in, first by giving the opting-in notice, and secondly as a separate step bearing in mind the wording of the section, by agreeing to do the shop work. Attention is drawn to the expression 'after giving that notice' contained in Sch 4, para 3(1)(b). An opting-in notice is defined in para 1(1) as having the meaning given to it in para 3(2) namely that it must—
  (a) be in writing;
  (b) be signed and dated by the shop worker;
  (c) expressly state that the shop worker wishes to work on Sunday; or
  (d) expressly state that he does not object to Sunday working.

A precedent for such a notice is set out in Appendix 2, Precedent 3.

11.39 It has been suggested for the reasons given at para 11.38 that it would not be sensible for the opting-in notice to include specific agreement to do shop work on Sundays. From a practical point of view it may be that the opting-in notice should be placed, signed, at the top of the page and the agreement to do specific shop work on Sundays could be placed underneath it and signed separately. There are clearly dangers however, in dealing with the matter in this way.

Opting-out

11.40 Having opted-in to Sunday shop work either by having served an opting-in notice or by having joined an employer who has agreed to work on Sundays, an employee has a right to opt-out of Sunday work. In order to opt-out a shop worker has to comply with the 1994 Act, Sch 4, para 4. He may at any time give his employer a notice which must—
  (a) be in writing;
  (b) be signed and dated by him; and
  (c) be to the effect that he objects to Sunday working.

11.41 Such a notice can only be given by a shop worker who, under his contract of employment, is or may be required to work on Sunday and is not a Sunday only worker. A Sunday only worker cannot for obvious and practical reasons opt-out. The opting-out notice does not have effect for a period of three months beginning with the day on which it was given (see Sch 4, para 6).

11.42 An opted-out shop worker is one falling within the meaning given to the expression by Sch 4, para 5(1). He is one who has given an opting-out notice and has been continuously employed from the date on which the notice was given until the appropriate date and he was employed as a shop worker throughout that period. By virtue of para 5(1)(c) specific provision is made so that if for part of the period concerned the shop worker was not employed under a contract of employment he shall not lose his protection as an opted-out shop worker provided he was a shop worker throughout the remainder of the time. Schedule 4, para 5(2) contains detailed

11.42 *Shop worker protection*

provisions as to what is the appropriate day. These provisions are in identical terms as to those who are protected shop workers (see paras 11.30 and 11.35).

Ceasing to be an opted-out shop worker

11.43 Schedule 4, para 5(5) provides the mechanics for ceasing to be an opted-out shop worker. These are the same as those for ceasing to be a protected shop worker. The worker concerned needs to give an opting-in notice, which will have the same information as the opting-in notice as discussed previously and he must expressly agree after giving the notice to do shop work on the Sunday or on a particular Sunday. (See Appendix 2, Precedent 4).

THE PROTECTION

11.44 *The first major protection given* to a protected or opted-out shop worker is the right not to be dismissed for refusing to do shop work on Sunday. Schedule 4, para 7(1) of the 1994 Act specifically provides that such dismissal shall be regarded for the purposes of Part V of the 1978 Act as unfair if the reason for it was that the shop worker refused, or proposed to refuse to do shop work on Sundays or on a particular Sunday. Paragraph 7 contains the usual provision that, in a case where there is more than one reason for dismissal, if the principle reason was the refusal to do shop work, the dismissal will be unfair.

11.45 However, this absolute protection is diminished slightly by the effects of para 7(2). This paragraph provides that the protection does not apply if the dismissal arose because the shop worker refused, or proposed to refuse, to do shop work on a Sunday or Sundays falling before the end of the three months notice period. However, para 7(3) provides that the dismissal will be unfair if the reason for it was that the shop worker had given or proposed to give an opting-out notice.

11.46 Similarly it will be unfair not to renew a fixed term contract on these grounds and the right to contract out of unfair dismissal protection given by s 142 of the 1978 Act cannot be used to contract out of the rights given not to be dismissed for refusing Sunday work.

11.47 *The second right specifically given* is a protection for redundant shop workers. If the dismissal of a protected or opted-out shop worker arises on the basis that the shop worker is redundant but the employee can show that he was selected for redundancy from a pool of other employees who held positions similar to him and that the reason for his selection was that he had refused or proposed to refuse to do shop work on Sunday or a particular Sunday then the dismissal shall be regarded as unfair.

11.48 However, as in the case of the first right given, that is not the case where the principle reason for selection was that the shop worker refused or proposed to refuse to do shop work on a Sunday or Sundays falling before the end of the opting-out notice period.

11.49 Similarly, in a redundancy selection situation as above, if the reason the shop worker was chosen for selection was that he gave or proposed to give an opting-out notice to the employer then that dismissal shall similarly be regarded as unfair.

Qualifying period and age limits

11.50 Perhaps one of the most significant concessions made to shop worker protection is that given by Sch 4, para 9 of the 1994 Act. This paragraph specifically disapplies the 1978 Act, ss 54, 64(1). These sections provide for a two year continuous employment period for full time employees before they become eligible to bring actions for unfair dismissal to an Industrial Tribunal and provide lower and upper age limits for such right and for compensation. These provisions do not apply to such dismissals under this Act. Hence, an employee may rely on the protections given however long he has worked for the retailer and irrespective of his age.

11.51 *The third right to be given* is that just as a protected or opted-out shop worker has the right not to be dismissed for refusing to do Sunday shop work, so by virtue of the detailed provisions of Sch 4, para 10 he has the right not to be subjected to any detriment. Detriment for this purpose means any act, or any deliberate failure to act by his employer. Such a detriment must occur because the shop worker refused, or proposed to refuse to do shop work on a Sunday or on a particular Sunday. Just as in the dismissal protection this does not apply in relation to an opted-out shop worker on the ground that he refused or proposed to refuse to do shop work on a Sunday or Sundays falling before the end of the notice period of three months. Similarly, as in the protection given against dismissal a shop worker must not be subjected to a detriment on the ground that he gave or proposed to give an opting-out notice.

11.52 These protections do not apply where the detriment in question amounts to dismissal where of course the employee has rights to complain to the Tribunal for unfair dismissal.

11.53 Schedule 4, para 10(5) of the 1994 Act sets out three cases in which potentially detrimental acts are not to be treated as detrimental for these purposes. First, it is not a detriment for the retailer to fail to pay remuneration in respect of Sunday shop work which the employee has not done. Secondly, it is not a detriment to fail to provide a shop worker with any other benefit where—
 (a) the shop worker has not done Sunday shop work;
 (b) the failure to provide the benefit results from an application of a contractual term under which the benefit varies according to the number of hours worked by the shop worker or his remuneration.

Thirdly, it is not a detriment to fail to provide the shop worker with any work, wage or any other benefit which the employer is not by virtue of Sch 4, paras 14 and 15 obliged to provide.

11.54 Paragraph 14 provides that subject to three conditions a protected shop worker's contract shall not be regarded as requiring the employer to provide the shop worker with shop work on weekdays in excess of the hours normally worked by the shop worker on weekdays before he ceased to do shop work on Sundays. These three conditions are—
 (a) that under the contract of employment of a shop worker who was a shop worker on the day before the commencement date (and not a Sunday only worker) the employer is or may be required to provide the shop worker with shop work for a specified number of hours each week.

11.54   Shop worker protection

(b) the shop worker was or might have been required to work on Sunday before the commencement date.

(c) the shop worker has done shop work on Sunday in that employment, whether or not before the commencement date but has, on or after that date, ceased to do so.

11.55   Thus it appears that Sch 4, para 14 takes a common sense approach to the problem of providing shop workers with additional hours of work should they cease to do Sunday work. If therefore a shop worker has worked on Sundays as part of the basic hours provided by his contract of employment, so that he has for instance only worked 32 hours a week from Monday to Saturday with a further five and a half hours on Sundays, then upon him ceasing to do Sunday work the employer cannot be asked to provide the shop worker with weekday hours over and above the 32 'normally worked' by him.

11.56   It is difficult to tell what the position will be in respect of provisions in the contract which provide for a specified number of hours to be worked, since historically the hours have been worked on varying days of the week; sometimes always on weekdays, whilst on other occasions on both weekdays and Sundays. No doubt this is a matter which Tribunals as arbiters of fact will find sensible ways of dealing with.

11.57   Schedule 4, para 15 deals with the same problem but from a slightly different perspective. It deals with a situation where a shop worker was on the commencement date required or might have been required to work on Sundays before that date and has done shop work on Sundays. Furthermore, the contract concerned does not make it clear what part of the remuneration payable, or any other benefit accruing to the shop worker was intended to be attributable, to shop work on Sundays.

11.58   There are many of these contracts in existence. Shop workers who are required to work on rotas which include Sundays and Bank Holidays are often paid at an enhanced rate of pay because built into the basic rate is a premium element for Sunday work and Bank Holiday work. That premium rate may not be apparent on the face of the contract.

11.59   In these situations para 15 provides that as long as the shop worker remains a protected shop worker, the employer may reduce the amount of pay by the proportion which the hours of shop work which the shop worker could have been required to work on Sundays bears to the aggregate of those hours and the hours of work actually done by the shop worker in the period.

11.60   It appears therefore that in these situations an employee who ceases to work on Sunday could continue to obtain some proportion of the premium rate built into such a contract. The message for employers is clear; their contracts must stipulate the amount of additional pay being paid for Sunday work, if any, so that if Sunday work ceases the employer can take away that premium element. If not they will be restricted to deducting a proportion in accordance with the formula set out in Sch 4, para 15.

11.61   Schedule 4, para 10(6) deals with another important practical issue, namely a situation where an employer offers to pay a sum to protected or opted-out shop workers who are not obliged by their contract to do shop work on Sundays in consideration for them doing such work on Sundays generally or on a particular Sunday.

11.62 In those situations no detriment is to be regarded as having accrued to an employer if the employer fails to make an offer or to pay that sum. Furthermore an employee who does not accept the offer is not to be regarded for those purposes as having been subjected to any detriment by any failure to pay him that sum.

11.63 What then are the remedies for an employee who suffers detriment as the result of his refusal to work on Sundays as set out in Sch 4, para 10? In Sch 4, para 16 an employee is given the same right which has been inserted into the 1978 Act by the Trade Union Reform and Employment Rights Act 1993 (TURERA 1993) in respect of health and safety cases, namely the right to apply to the Tribunal for compensation.

11.64 Section 22B of the 1978 Act which allows an employee to present a complaint to an Industrial Tribunal on the ground he has been subjected to a detriment is amended to allow a complaint for a contravention of Sch 4, para 10 of the 1994 Act. With such a complaint the onus is on the employer to show the ground on which any act, or deliberate failure to act, was done. Any complaint must be made before the end of three months beginning with the date of the act or the failure to act or, where the act or failure is part of a similar series, the last of them.

11.65 There is also the usual provision which enables a Tribunal to deal with the matter out of time if it was not 'reasonably practicable' for the complaint to have been presented before the end of that period. Section 22C of the 1978 Act enables the Tribunal, if it finds that the complaint was well founded, to make a declaration to that effect and to make an award of compensation to the complainant in respect of the act or failure to act.

11.66 The amount of the compensation shall be such as the Tribunal considers just and equitable in the circumstances having regard to the infringement and to any loss which is attributable to the act or failure, including any expenses incurred and any loss of benefit.

11.67 The Tribunal expects and must take into account the duty of the employee to mitigate his losses and may reduce the amount of compensation by a proportion it considers just and equitable regarding the extent to which the employee caused or contributed to that detriment. In addition to the right in connection with detriment cases Sch 4, para 19 provides that the 1978 Act, s 60A shall now include a reference to the 1994 Act, Sch 4.

11.68 Section 60A of the 1978 Act, which deals with the dismissal on the grounds of assertion of a statutory right, provides that the dismissal of an employee is regarded as unfair if the employee has brought proceedings against the employer to enforce a right, in this case, under the 1994 Act, or alleges that the employee has infringed a right under the 1994 Act. It is immaterial whether a right has or has not in fact been infringed but the employer must have brought the claim in good faith. It is quite sufficient that the employee makes it reasonably clear to the employer what the right claimed to have been infringed was.

11.69 This new head of unfair dismissal was also introduced by TURERA 1993 as part of the Government's Citizens' Charter. The protection offered is very strong. Any dismissal contrary to the section is automatically unfair as is any selection for redundancy on those grounds.

11.70 *Shop worker protection*

BURDEN OF PROOF

11.70   It is perhaps sensible to consider how easy it will be for shop workers to prove that which they allege before an Industrial Tribunal.

11.71   It appears that there may be a difference in the burden of proof depending on whether the employee in question has more or less than two years' continuous service. It may be sensible to consider the case law concerning dismissal for trade union related reasons. It has been suggested that if the employee has less than two years' service he will face the normal civil burden of proving their case on the balance of probability.[1] Even with two years' continuous employment, although the burden is upon the employer initially to show the reasons for dismissal, having put forward his reasons in effect it is then for the employee to disprove these.

[1]   *Smith v Hayle Town Council* [1978] 1 ICR 996, CA.

MISCELLANEOUS PROVISIONS

11.72   In Sch 4 of the 1994 Act there are a number of other provisions which apply or disapply the provisions of the 1978 Act.

11.73   Paragraph 17 deals with the restrictions on contracting out of the other provisions of Sch 4 of the 1994 Act. Any such provision whether contained in a contract of employment or elsewhere is void insofar as it excludes or limits the provisions of the Schedule or precludes any person from making a complaint to the Industrial Tribunal. However, these restrictions do not apply to an agreement where ACAS have taken action to conciliate in a dispute or in the case of unfair dismissal or where the conditions regulating compromise agreements under the 1978 Act are satisfied.

11.74   Paragraph 20 provides that it is not possible to contract out of the jurisdiction of the Industrial Tribunal for Sunday trading cases in dismissal procedure agreements.

11.75   Paragraph 18 provides transitional modifications relating to maternity cases. The effect of the detailed provisions of the paragraph is to ensure that where an employee exercises the right to return to work, she shall have all the protections given by Part IV of the 1950 Act even though her contract of employment may have expired or terminated as if she was still employed under her original contract of employment provided she was a shop worker and not a Sunday only worker.

11.76   Paragraph 21 gives ACAS all of the statutory powers to effect conciliation of disputes as for other types of unfair dismissal.

11.77   Paragraph 22 provides that when interpreting the 1978 Act, ss 129, 141(2), 150, Sch 12, any reference therein to Part II of the 1978 Act shall include a reference to the 1994 Act, Sch 4, para 10. These provisions relate first in s 129 to the provision that any dispute must be resolved by way of complaint or reference to the Industrial Tribunal and not otherwise. Section 141(2) relates to employment outside the UK. The effect is that a shop worker who is employed ordinarily to work outside Great Britain will not have the protection given by the Act. Section 150 and Sch 12 which deal with provisions relating to the death of the employee or the employer will apply to issues arising under Sch 4 of the 1994 Act. Sch 4, para 10 of the 1994 Act relates to the power relating to detriment.

Duty to give explanatory statement

11.78   Schedule 4, para 11 imposes a statutory duty on an employer to provide a shop worker before the end of two months with a written statement in the prescribed form. The paragraph applies to shop workers who are not Sunday only workers who under their contracts are or may be required to work on Sundays (whether or not as a result of giving an opting-in notice).

11.79   Thus it is apparent that the explanatory statement must be given—
   (a)   to all existing shop workers who cease to be protected by opting-in to Sunday work;
   (b)   to all new shop workers who at the commencement of their employment are obliged to work on Sundays or who become so obliged by virtue of having opted-in and agree to do Sunday work.

11.80   The remedy given for a failure of the employer's duty is that the employee who has not been made aware of his rights is only required to give one month's notice of his intention to opt-out of Sunday work rather than three months' notice. This protection may therefore be somewhat illusory bearing in mind he may not be aware of his rights because of the failure to provide him with the prescribed form.

11.81   However, an employer is not required to give the statement in the situation where during the two month period the shop worker has given an opting-out notice. The form is prescribed and is set out in para 11(4). It may be amended by order of the Secretary of State. The 1994 Act does not appear to oblige employers to provide the notice in the language of the employee.

Contracts of employment and Schedule 4

11.82   Schedule 4, paras 12–15 deal with the effect of Part IV of the 1950 Act on the rights on contracts of employment. These paragraphs are fundamental to the protection which is given to shop workers. First, any contract of employment under which a protected shop worker is required to do shop work on Sunday on or after the commencement date or which alternatively requires the employer to provide shop work to the shop worker on Sunday on or after that day is unenforceable to that extent. Similarly any agreement entered into after the commencement date between a protected shop worker and his employer is unenforceable in the same way.

11.83   By virtue of Sch 4, para 12(3) once a protected shop worker opts-in and expressly agrees to do Sunday shop work and thus ceases to be protected, his contract of employment is deemed to have been varied to the extent necessary to give effect to the terms of the agreement. By virtue of paragraph 12(4) the same protection is given to shop workers returning from maternity leave.

11.84   Schedule 4, para 13 contains similar provisions. Once he has opted-out a shop worker's contract of employment becomes unenforceable to the extent that it requires the opted-out shop worker to do Sunday work or his employer to provide that work. Similarly any agreement entered into after opting-out is unenforceable in the same way.

11.85 *Shop worker protection*

11.85 However, once he has opted-in again the opted-out shop worker's contract of employment is again taken to be varied to the extent necessary to give effect to the terms of Sunday work which has been agreed. There are similar provisions as to maternity leavers.

11.86 Paragraph 14, as previously explained, provides that for as long as the shop worker is a protected shop worker, his contract shall not be regarded as requiring the employer to provide him with shop work on weekdays in excess of the hours normally worked by him before he ceased to do Sunday shop work. Similarly para 15 makes provisions for determining the rates of pay to be paid to shop workers when they have ceased to do Sunday shop work.

THE SHRC/USDAW UNDERTAKINGS

11.87 In the course of the political campaign, the major retailers who made up the SHRC entered into a number of undertakings with USDAW. They are set out in this section of this Chapter as they will be a valuable aid to employers and employees of those companies in understanding their commitments to introducing full employee protection and in particular the obligation to incorporate into employees' contracts of employment all of the rights contained in Sch 4.

11.88 The undertakings given were as follows—
  (a) *Premium pay*. That the companies will continue to pay current premium rates of pay to Sunday employees. They will only deviate from this if there is a significant change in the circumstances in which retail work is rewarded and only after appropriate consultation. The companies recognise that a premium will be required to attract sufficient high quality employees for Sunday work.
  (b) *Opting-out notice*. That the companies would only require employees to give one month's notice of their intention to opt out of Sunday work.
  (c) *Contracts of employment*. That the companies would incorporate the right to opt out of Sunday work into employees' terms and conditions of employment.
  (d) *Communication of shopworker rights*. That the companies would endeavour to make the opting-out procedure as simple as possible, by providing clear forms to employees and by pursuing an effective communications strategy to make employees aware of their rights by such means as posters in staff rest rooms and canteens, and articles written for in-house journals and inclusion in the staff handbook.
  (e) *Lost working hours*. That where an existing shopworker opts out of Sunday work the companies will use their best endeavour to reschedule the employee's lost working hours elsewhere subject to the needs of the business.
  (f) *Standard working week*. The standard working week for shop floor employees shall not exceed 39 hours and hours worked in excess of this will be paid at currently agreed rates.

SOME POSSIBLE DEFECTS IN THE PROTECTION GIVEN TO SHOP WORKERS WORKING ON SUNDAYS

11.89 A shop worker is only protected if he is a shop worker on 25 August 1994. If he was to be dismissed some days before the commencement date and then offered re-employment on or after the commencement date he would not be so protected. It has been suggested that there is nothing in the Act which compels the employer to notify his employees that they are under no legal obligation to sign opting-in forms or that they should be paid for their agreement to do so. There is also nothing in the 1994 Act which provides for premium pay on Sundays.

11.90 It is clear that to be protected an employee must be employed under a contract of employment. However, there is no protection given to people engaged under contracts for services. This could be a serious exclusion as it applies to many particularly vulnerable groups of workers such as casual workers who may not be categorised as employees. Despite efforts in the passage of the Bill to extend the protection to 'workers' as defined by the Wages Act 1986, no such extension occurred. During the course of the debate in Parliament much also was made of the failures of the Industrial Tribunal system generally.[1]

---

1   HL 3R, 19 May 1994, col 448.

12 Existing Sunday work protection

BACKGROUND

12.1 Although it appears that the courts and Industrial Tribunals do not recognise the existence of any rights to refuse to work on Sundays provided there is a contractual obligation to do so, they will of course give protection to those who have no such contractual obligation. However, a worker with less than two years' continuous employment has no protection under EC law against being compelled to work on Sundays.[1]

---

[1] *Steadman v Hogg-Robinson Ltd* EAT 794/93 (unreported).

12.2 The dismissal by the employer because of the employee's refusal to do Sunday work where there is no contractual obligation to do so is likely in most cases, where the employee has the relevant qualifying period of employment, to constitute a constructive dismissal. The fairness of such dismissal will depend on the reasons for the employer's request for Sunday work and the reasons for the employee's refusal. The working of excessive hours including Sundays may also constitute grounds for resignation and a claim for unfair constructive dismissal.[1]

---

[1] *George v PBI (International) Ltd*, Bury St Edmunds Industrial Tribunal, 3 October 1991, Case No COIT 29560/90.

12.3 However, for workers in the retail sector, the Shops Act 1950, s 22, re-enacting the earlier provisions of the Shops Act 1936, contains substantial protection for shop workers who work on Sundays.

12.4 The Deregulation and Contracting Out Bill currently contains no provision repealing s 22 although at Committee Stage in the House of Lords there was an attempt to introduce such an amendment. This was withdrawn on the Government's undertaking to consider the issue further and bring it back during the course of the Parliamentary progress of that Bill. However, the Sunday Trading Act 1994 specifically amends s 22 and it must therefore be considered that it will continue to have statutory effect for some time.

SHOPS ACT 1950, S 22

12.5 Section 22 of the 1950 Act provides—

'(1) No person shall be employed on Sunday about the business of a shop which is open for the serving of customers unless the following requirements are complied with—
    (a) in the case of a person so employed for more than four hours on any Sunday, that person shall—

(i) receive in respect of his employment on that Sunday a whole holiday on a day other than that of his statutory half-holiday, if any, and that whole holiday shall be on a weekday of the week beginning with that Sunday unless he has, in respect of his employment on that Sunday, already received such a holiday on a weekday of the previous week;

(ii) not be employed about the business of a shop on more than two other Sundays in the same month;

(b) in the case of a person not so employed for more than four hours on a Sunday in any month, that person shall receive in respect of his employment on any Sunday in the month a half-holiday in addition to his statutory half-holiday, if any, and that additional half-holiday shall be on a weekday of the week beginning with that Sunday unless he has, in respect of his employment on that Sunday, already received such a half-holiday on a weekday of the previous week—

Provided that this subsection shall not apply—

(i) to any person employed wholly or mainly in connection with the sale of intoxicating liquor; or

(ii) to any shop assistant employed in any premises for the sale of refreshments to whom the provisions of paragraphs (a), (b), (c) and (d) of subsection (3) of the last foregoing section apply by virtue of an election made under that section by the occupier of the premises; or

(iii) to any person employed wholly or mainly as a milk roundsman; or

(iv) to any person employed in the transaction of post office business; or

(v) to any registered pharmacist within the meaning of the Pharmacy and Poisons Act 1933 employed in connection with the sale or supply of medicines or medical or surgical appliances in any premises required to be kept open on Sunday for the serving of customers in pursuance of a contract between the occupier of the premises and a Family Practitioner Committee—

(a) if he is not employed for more than two hours on that Sunday, and has not been employed on the previous Sunday, and

(b) if on a weekday (other than the day of the statutory half-holiday) of the previous week or of the week commencing with the Sunday on which he is so employed, either he has not been, or will not be, employed before half past ten o'clock in the morning, or has not been, or will not be, employed after six o'clock in the afternoon.

(2) For the purposes of this section—

(a) a person who works about the business of a shop for the occupier thereof shall be deemed to be employed notwithstanding that he receives no reward for his labour;

(b) in relation to any person employed about the business of a shop the following expressions have the meanings hereby respectively assigned to them, that is to say,

12.5 Existing Sunday work protection

"whole holiday" means a day on which that person is not employed about the business of that shop;

"statutory half-holiday" means a day on which under section seventeen of this Act he is not employed about the business of that shop after half-past one in the afternoon;

"half-holiday" means a day on which he is either not employed before, or not employed after, half-past one o'clock in the afternoon of that day about the business of the shop.

(3) The occupier of any shop which [is lawfully][1] open for the serving of customers on Sunday shall keep in the prescribed form and in the prescribed manner a record of the names of and the hours worked by all the persons employed about the business of the shop on Sunday who are entitled to any holidays prescribed by this section, and of the respective days of the week upon which those persons receive those holidays.

(4) Nothing in this section shall authorise the employment of any person at any time when it would under any other provision of this Act or under section 9 of the Cinemas Act 1985, be unlawful for him to be so employed.

(5) Nothing in this section shall apply to the carrying on on Sunday of the business of a retail dealer in butchers' meat.

(6) In the case of any contravention of this section, the occupier of the shop shall be liable to a fine not exceeding level 2 on the standard scale.

(7) This section shall not extend to Scotland.'

---

[1] Words in square brackets substituted by the 1994 Act, Sch 4, para 23.

12.6 As can be seen this section imposes criminal liabilities on employers but it is presumed that a breach of s 22 by an employer by either insisting that the employee worked for more than three Sundays in every month or refusing to allow the employee a day off during the week might also constitute a constructive dismissal.

12.7 What then is included in s 22? First, it is apparent that an employer has an obligation to keep records in the statutory form. Secondly, it is apparent that employees must receive a statutory holiday during the week before or the week after the Sunday in which they have worked, and finally it is apparent that such employees may only work for three Sundays in any one month.

12.8 Who then has the benefit of the statutory protection given by s 22? Section 22 provides that protection is given to those employees 'employed on Sunday about the business of a shop'. As has been discussed previously in Chapter 2, the 1950 Act, s 74(1) defines a 'shop' as 'including premises where any retail trade or business is carried on' and similarly it is apparent from s 22 that 'retail trade or business' has a very wide meaning.

12.9 Therefore the most important question is how to construe the words 'about the business of a shop'? Case law on the subject shows that the words are to be given a very wide construction.[1]

---

[1] *George v James* [1914] KB 278 and *London County Council v Wettman* [1922] 1 KB 143.

12.10 From the cases it is apparent that it is necessary to look at the whole business of the shop, including business which was done outside the actual premises. The courts had to construe the words liberally to prevent evasion of the Act.

12.11   It has been suggested that the test may be that any one who acts for the shop for the purpose of advancing the ultimate goal of selling its goods, acts about the business of a shop, and it may make no difference therefore whether that person works within the shop or elsewhere. For these purposes therefore the protection given by s 22 may be given to a wider class of people than that given by the Sunday Trading Act 1994, Sch 4 itself. Taking this approach, it appears that delivery drivers and warehouse employees stationed at a shop are likely to be included. Catering staff in an in-house restaurant and office staff are also going to be included.

12.12   It is arguable that some head office staff engaged in ordering and distribution etc also work about the business of a shop, and those involved in distribution of goods to the store may also be protected. However, does the protection given by s 22 extend to part time staff alone? The intention of the legislation appears to be to ensure that a worker had a day free from work during the week if he works in excess of four hours on Sundays.

12.13   Part time staff or Sunday only staff in any event receive a day in which they are not employed about the business of the shop. The author would argue that they were not covered by s 22.

The statutory record

12.14   The Shops Act 1950, s 22 provides that the employer is obliged to keep a record at the shop in a prescribed form recording the names of the employees and the hours worked by all persons employed about the business of the shop on Sunday who are entitled to any holidays, and the days of the week upon which they receive those holidays. The form of the record is contained in the Shops Regulations 1937, SI 1937/271. The form has long ceased to be supplied by HMSO but to aid readers it is reproduced in Appendix 2, Precedent 6.

12.15   The Regulations require the records to be made on the day to which they relate or if this is not reasonably practical on the day after. The obligation is clearly to produce a record containing the necessary information in the required format. This duty is specifically referred to in the Sunday Trading Act. Schedule 4, para 23 amends s 22(3) consequent upon the repeal of the 1950 Act, ss 47–66. It is therefore clear that the 1994 Act retains the duty to keep records.

12.16   It appears therefore that records must be kept of all workers who work weekdays and Sundays and who are entitled to the appropriate holidays. Not to do so is an offence prosecutable by the local authority which bears a maximum fine at level 2 on the standard scale.

Holiday in compensation for Sunday work

12.17   These provisions provide that where a worker works on Sundays for more than four hours he must receive a whole day's holiday in a weekday either in the week before or the week after the Sunday in question. For those who work for less than four hours on a Sunday, a half day holiday alone is required. It must be stressed that the entitlement is for holiday and there is no requirement that this must be paid holiday.

12.18   The question arises as to whether this right can be given up voluntarily by the employee especially after the commencement of the Sunday Trading Act and

12.18 *Existing Sunday work protection*

employees are entitled to give their employer opting-in and opting-out notices. This has been the subject of previous litigation[1] in which it is clear that the duty is upon the employer to ensure that the employee takes these days as holiday and this right cannot be given up voluntarily by the employee.

---
[1] *Ward v Smith (WH) & Son* [1913] 3 KB 154.

Three Sundays in any month

12.19 The same class of people, ie those who work on weekdays and Sundays, may only work for three Sundays in four. Similarly it appears that they cannot give up that right voluntarily.

Conclusion

12.20 The provisions of s 22 are cumbersome and employers and employees have had difficulties in complying with them for many years. There has been little enforcement by local authorities who have taken the pragmatic view that the production of records, although not necessarily in the statutory form, showing that the Act has been complied with, has been sufficient for the purposes of the Act. If s 22 remains in existence in the future and is not repealed by the Deregulation and Contracting Out Bill, employers and employees will have to accept that the number of Sundays which can be worked are limited by statute and that time must be given in lieu of Sunday work.

OTHER STATUTORY PROTECTION

12.21 It is worth commenting upon the provisions for break periods contained in the 1950 Act, s 19 which also remains unrepealed by the 1994 Act.

12.22 Section 19 provides that intervals for meals shall be allowed for each shop assistant in accordance with Pt I of Sch 3 to the 1950 Act. It does not apply to family shops where shop assistants are members of the family of the occupier who are both maintained by him and live in his house. Other than this exception, it applies to all shop assistants.

12.23 A shop assistant is defined by the 1950 Act as a considerably narrower class of employee than that referred to in s 22. Shop assistants are defined by s 74 as 'any person wholly or mainly employed in a shop in connection with the serving of customers or the receipt of orders or the despatch of goods'.

12.24 It appears therefore that this primarily relates to catering staff and shop floor assistants and will not cover warehouse workers, office workers, head office workers, transport workers or managerial staff in stores. For such employees the following rights exist—

    (a) no shop worker shall be employed for more than six hours without a 20 minute interval in the course of it;

(b) without prejudice to the general right at para (a) above, for shop workers who work between 11.30am and 2.30pm an interval of not less than three quarters of an hour shall be allowed;
(c) where the hours of employment include the hours from 4.00pm to 7.00pm an interval of not less than half an hour shall be allowed between those hours for tea;
(d) the interval allowed for lunch at para (b) above is increased to one hour if the meal is taken away from the shop;
(e) special dispensation is given for those who work in cafés, restaurants, off licences and public houses who may be given their lunch time break either before 11.30am or at 2.30pm.

12.25 These are also important statutory provisions which continue to affect all employees who work on Sundays after the commencement of the 1994 Act whether in large or small shops within the meaning of the Act.

13 Repeals

BACKGROUND

13.1 The Sunday Trading Act 1994 is one of two measures which during 1994 will revolutionise shopping hours in England and Wales. The second measure, the Deregulation and Contracting Out Bill (which will also affect Scotland), will abolish the restrictions on weekday shopping hours contained in the Shops Act 1950, Pt I, if it is enacted. In this Chapter the repeals set out in the 1994 Act are examined and the remaining provisions of the 1950 Act are commented on.

REPEALS

13.2 By virtue of s 1(2) of the 1994 Act, Pt IV (ss 47–66) of the 1950 Act, which governs Sunday trading, ceases to have effect on the appointed day, which has been designated 26 August 1994. Similarly the Fifth Schedule (the goods which are permitted to be sold on Sundays under the 1950 Act), the Sixth Schedule, (the goods which could be sold on Sundays under a partial exemption order) and the Seventh Schedule (the goods which could be sold on Sundays in holiday resorts) are all repealed with effect from 26 August 1994.

13.3 By virtue of s 6 of the 1994 Act power is given to the Secretary of State by statutory instrument to either amend or repeal any provision of any local Act, which appears to him to be inconsistent with or rendered unnecessary by the 1994 Act.[1] However, the Secretary of State must consult first with the local authority before he makes such an order.

---

[1] For examples of such local Acts see the Tyne and Wear Act 1976, the West Midlands County Council Act 1980, the Greater London Council (General Powers) Act 1981 and the Greater London Council (General Powers) Act 1983.

13.4 Schedule 4, para 24 of the 1994 Act repeals the Children and Young Persons Act 1933, s 20(3), which provided that bylaws may not authorise a child to be engaged or employed on a Sunday in street trading.

PROPOSED REPEALS UNDER THE DEREGULATION AND CONTRACTING OUT BILL

13.5 Under the Deregulation and Contracting Out Bill (as it currently stands) the 1950 Act, Part I (ss 1–16) and ss 40–43, together with s 70 and the First, Second and Fourth Schedules are to be repealed.

13.6 Consequential amendments will be made to ss 44, 45, 46, 67(4), 69(1), 71(1) and 74(1). The Shops (Airports) Act 1962 and the Shops (Early Closing Days) Act 1965 will be repealed.

13.7 Therefore little will be left of the 1950 Act but the following sections will still remain in force, namely—
  (a) sections 22, 18 and the Third Schedule (as to which see Chapter 12);
  (b) section 71 which imposes the duty on local authorities to enforce the Act insofar as it remains; and
  (c) section 67 which regulates the business of hairdressers and barbers in Scotland on Sundays.

OTHER REPEALS

13.8 The Sunday Trading Act 1994, Sch 5 contains specific repeals some of which have already been mentioned. For the sake of completeness these provisions are now specifically dealt with. As previously mentioned the Children and Young Persons Act 1933, s 20(3) has been repealed as well as the Children and Young Persons Act 1963, s 35(3) which also relates to the employment of children for street trading on Sundays. In the 1950 Act ss 47–66 are repealed as are the words 'or Part IV' in s 71(7)(b) and the whole of the Fifth, Sixth and Seventh Schedules. The Shops (Airports) Act 1962, s 1(1) is amended. As will be appreciated however, this Act will be repealed by the Deregulation Bill. The London Government Act 1963, s 51(3) has been repealed. This provision, which dealt with the powers contained in the 1950 Act, s 54, giving special provisions for London, is repealed as a consequence of the repeal of s 54. An amendment is made to the Post Office Act 1969, Sch 4 which extended the meaning of post office business so far as it related to s 22 of the 1950 Act (Sunday employment), s 44 (exemptions for Post Office business) and Schs 2 and 5. In the Airports Act 1986, s 70 and Sch 5, para 15 are repealed. Finally the Employment Act 1989, Sch 3, Pt III, para 2(c) is repealed.

CONCLUSION

13.9 Whether the Sunday Trading Act 1994 will produce permanent, practical and popular law as claimed by its supporters, and in particular the Shopping Hours Reform Council, remains to be seen. What is apparent is that the trading provisions discussed in Chapters 1–10 of this book are relatively clear and should with a few exceptions leave little room for litigation.

13.10 However, it appears that the new shop worker protection measures together with the measures which already are in existence in the 1950 Act, ss 18, 22 as described in Chapters 11 and 12 respectively may well lead to a growth in Industrial Tribunal cases on this subject.

Appendix 1

Sunday Trading Act 1994

Sunday Trading Act 1994

(1994 c 20)

ARRANGEMENT OF SECTIONS

Section
1 Reform of law relating to Sunday trading
2 Loading and unloading at large shops on Sunday morning
3 Construction of certain leases and agreements
4 Rights of shop workers as respects Sunday working
5 Exclusion of Part I of Shops Act 1950
6 Consequential repeal or amendment of local Acts
7 Expenses
8 Meaning of "local authority"
9 Short title, repeals, commencement and extent

SCHEDULES
    Schedule 1—Restrictions on Sunday opening of large shops
    Schedule 2—Supplementary provisions
        Part I—General enforcement provisions
        Part II—Shops occupied by persons observing the Jewish Sabbath
    Schedule 3—Loading and unloading at large shops on Sunday morning
    Schedule 4—Rights of shop workers as respects Sunday working
    Schedule 5—Repeals

An Act to reform the law of England and Wales relating to Sunday trading; to make provision as to the rights of shop workers under the law of England and Wales in relation to Sunday working; and for connected purposes.

[5 July 1994]

Parliamentary debates.
House of Commons:
2nd Reading 29 November 1993: 233 HC Official Report (6th series) col 819.
Committee 8 December 1993: 234 HC Official Report (6th series) col 326, 9 February 1994: 237 HC Official Report (6th series) col 388.
Committee 13–25 January 1994: HC Official Report, SC A (Sunday Trading Bill).
Remaining Stages 23 February 1994: 238 HC Official Report (6th series) col 283.
Lords' Amendments 21 June 1994: 118 HC Official Report (6th series) col 154.
House of Lords:
2nd Reading 8 March 1994: 550 HL Official Report (5th series) col 1340.
Committee 29 March 1994: 553 HL Official Report (5th series) col 983, 14 April 1994: 553 HL Official Report (5th series) col 1623, 18 April 1994: 554 HL Official Report (5th series) col 9.
Report 5 May 1994: 554 HL Official Report (5th series) col 1218.
3rd Reading 19 May 1994: HL Official Report (5th series) col 418.
Commons' Amendments 30 June 1994: 556 HL Official Report (5th series) col 154.

1 Reform of law relating to Sunday trading

(1) Schedules 1 and 2 to this Act shall come into force on such day as the Secretary of State may by order made by statutory instrument appoint (in this section referred to as "the appointed day").

(2) Sections 47 to 66 of, and Schedules 5, 6 and 7 to, the Shops Act 1950 shall cease to have effect on the appointed day.

Appointed day 26 August 1994 (SI 1994/1841).
References See para 1.36.

2 Loading and unloading at large shops on Sunday morning

(1) A local authority may by resolution designate their area as a loading control area for the purposes of this section with effect from a date specified in the resolution, which must be a date at least one month after the date on which the resolution is passed.

(2) A local authority may by resolution revoke any designation made by them under subsection (1) above.

(3) It shall be the duty of a local authority, before making or revoking any designation under subsection (1) above, to consult persons appearing to the local authority to be likely to be affected by the proposed designation or revocation (whether as the occupiers of shops or as local residents) or persons appearing to the local authority to represent such persons.

(4) Where a local authority make or revoke a designation under this section, they shall publish notice of the designation or revocation in such manner as they consider appropriate.

(5) Schedule 3 to this Act (which imposes restrictions on loading and unloading on Sunday before 9 am at large shops in loading control areas) shall have effect.

References See Chapter 6.

3 Construction of certain leases and agreements

(1) Where any lease or agreement (however worded) entered into before the commencement of this section has the effect of requiring the occupier of a shop to keep the shop open for the serving of retail customers—
    (a) during normal business hours, or
    (b) during hours to be determined otherwise than by or with the consent of the occupier,
that lease or agreement shall not be regarded as requiring, or as enabling any person to require, the occupier to open the shop on Sunday for the serving of retail customers.

(2) Subsection (1) above shall not affect any lease or agreement—
    (a) to the extent that it relates specifically to Sunday and would (apart from this section) have the effect of requiring Sunday trading of a kind which before the commencement of this section would have been lawful by virtue of any provision of Part IV of the Shops Act 1950, or
    (b) to the extent that it is varied by agreement after the commencement of this section.

(3) In this section "retail customer" and "shop" have the same meaning as in Schedule 1 to this Act.

References See Chapter 7.

4 Rights of shop workers as respects Sunday working

Schedule 4 to this Act shall have effect.

References See Chapters 11 and 12.

5 Exclusion of Part I of Shops Act 1950

(1) Part I of the Shops Act 1950 (hours of closing) shall not apply on Sunday.

(2) In section 3 of that Act (by virtue of which Saturday is to be the late day unless the local authority by order fix some other day) for "some other day" there shall be substituted "some other week day".

(3) In section 12 of that Act (trading elsewhere than in shops) after "at any time" there shall be inserted "on a week day".

References See Chapter 3.

6 Consequential repeal or amendment of local Acts

(1) The Secretary of State may by order made by statutory instrument—
   (a) repeal any provision of a local Act passed before or in the same Session as this Act if it appears to him that the provision is inconsistent with or has become unnecessary in consequence of any provision of this Act, and
   (b) amend any provision of such a local Act if it appears to him that the provision requires amendment in consequence of any provision of this Act or any repeal made by virtue of paragraph (a) above.

(2) It shall be the duty of the Secretary of State, before he makes an order under subsection (1) above repealing or amending any provision of a local Act, to consult each local authority which he considers would be affected by the repeal or amendment of that provision.

(3) A statutory instrument containing an order under subsection (1) above shall be subject to annulment in pursuance of a resolution of either House of Parliament.

References See Chapter 13.

7 Expenses

There shall be paid out of money provided by Parliament any increase attributable to this Act in the sums payable out of such money under any other Act.

8 Meaning of "local authority"

(1) In this Act "local authority" means any unitary authority or any district council so far as they are not a unitary authority.

(2) In subsection (1) above "unitary authority" means—
   (a) the council of any county so far as they are the council for an area for which there are no district councils,
   (b) the council of any district comprised in an areas for which there is no county council,
   (c) a county borough council,
   (d) a London borough council,
   (e) the Common Council of the City of London, or
   (f) the Council of the Isles of Scilly.

(3) Until 1st April 1996, the definition of "unitary authority" in subsection (2) above shall have effect with the omission of paragraph (c).

References See Chapter 9.

9 Short title, repeals, commencement and extent

(1) This Act may be cited as the Sunday Trading Act 1994.

(2) The enactments mentioned in Schedule 5 to this Act are hereby repealed to the extent specified in the third column of that Schedule.

(3) The following provisions of this Act—
sections 2 to 5,
subsection (2) of this section, and
Schedules 3, 4 and 5,

shall not come into force until the appointed day (as defined in section 1 above).

(4) This Act extends to England and Wales only.

References See Chapter 13.

SCHEDULES

SCHEDULE 1

Section 1(1)

RESTRICTIONS ON SUNDAY OPENING OF LARGE SHOPS

Interpretation

1. In this Schedule—
"intoxicating liquor" has the same meaning as in the Licensing Act 1964,
"large shop" means a shop which has a relevant floor area exceeding 280 square metres,
"medicinal product" and "registered pharmacy" have the same meaning as in the Medicines Act 1968,
"relevant floor area", in relation to a shop, means the internal floor area of so much of the shop as consists of or is comprised in a building, but excluding any part of the shop which, throughout the week ending with the Sunday in question, is used neither for the serving of customers in connection with the sale of goods nor for the display of goods,
"retail customer" means a person who purchases goods retail,
"retail sale" means any sale other than a sale for use or resale in the course of a trade or business, and references to retail purchase shall be construed accordingly,
"sale of goods" does not include—
  (a) the sale of meals, refreshments or intoxicating liquor for consumption on the premises on which they are sold, or
  (b) the sale of meals or refreshments prepared to order for immediate consumption off those premises,
"shop" means any premises where there is carried on a trade or business consisting wholly or mainly of the sale of goods, and
"stand", in relation to an exhibition, means any platform, structure, space or other area provided for exhibition purposes.

Large shops not to open on Sunday except in accordance with notice to local authority

2.—(1) Subject to sub-paragraphs (2) and (3) below, a large shop shall not be open on Sunday for the serving of retail customers.

(2) Sub-paragraph (1) above does not apply in relation to—
  (a) any of the shops mentioned in paragraph 3(1) below, or
  (b) any shop in respect of which a notice under paragraph 8(1) of Schedule 2 to this Act (shops occupied by persons observing the Jewish Sabbath) has effect.

(3) Where a notice under paragraph 4 below has effect in relation to a shop, sub-paragraph (1) above does not apply in relation to the shop during the permitted Sunday opening hours specified in the notice, but this sub-paragraph has effect subject to sub-paragraph (4) below.

(4) The exemption conferred by sub-paragraph (3) above does not apply where the Sunday is Easter Day or Christmas Day.

Exemptions

3.—(1) The shops referred to in paragraph 2(2)(a) above are—
- (a) any shop which is at a farm and where the trade or business carried on consists wholly or mainly of the sale of produce from that farm,
- (b) any shop where the trade or business carried on consists wholly or mainly of the sale of intoxicating liquor,
- (c) any shop where the trade or business carried on consists wholly or mainly of the sale of any one or more of the following—
  - (i) motor supplies and accessories, and
  - (ii) cycle supplies and accessories,
- (d) any shop which—
  - (i) is a registered pharmacy, and
  - (ii) is not open for the retail sale of any goods other than medicinal products and medical and surgical appliances,
- (e) any shop at a designated airport which is situated in a part of the airport to which sub-paragraph (3) below applies,
- (f) any shop in a railway station,
- (g) any shop at a service area within the meaning of the Highways Act 1980,
- (h) any petrol filling station,
- (j) any shop which is not open for the retail sale of any goods other than food, stores or other necessaries required by any person for a vessel or aircraft on its arrival at, or immediately before its departure from, a port, harbour or airport, and
- (k) any stand used for the retail sale of goods during the course of an exhibition.

(2) In determining whether a shop falls within sub-paragraph (1)(a), (b) or (c) above, regard shall be had to the nature of the trade or business carried on there on weekdays as well as to the nature of the trade or business carried on there on Sunday.

(3) This sub-paragraph applies to every part of a designated airport, except any part which is not ordinarily used by persons travelling by air to or from the airport.

(4) In this paragraph "designated airport" means an airport designated for the purposes of this paragraph by an order made by the Secretary of State, as being an airport at which there appears to him to be a substantial amount of international passenger traffic.

(5) The power to make an order under sub-paragraph (4) above shall be exercisable by statutory instrument.

(6) Any order made under section 1(2) of the Shops (Airports) Act 1962 and in force at the commencement of this Schedule shall, so far as it relates to England and Wales, have effect as if made also under sub-paragraph (4) above, and may be amended or revoked as it has effect for the purposes of this paragraph by an order under sub-paragraph (4) above.

Notice of proposed Sunday opening

4.—(1) A person who is, or proposes to become, the occupier of a large shop may give notice to the local authority for the area in which the shop is situated—
- (a) stating that he proposes to open the shop on Sunday for the serving of retail customers, and
- (b) specifying a continuous period of six hours, beginning no earlier than 10 am and ending no later than 6 pm, as the permitted Sunday opening hours in relation to the shop.

(2) The occupier of a shop in respect of which notice has been given under sub-paragraph (1) above may, by a subsequent notice—
- (a) specify permitted Sunday opening hours that could be specified under sub-paragraph (1)(b) above but are different from those specified in the earlier notice, or
- (b) cancel the earlier notice.

(3) A notice under this paragraph shall not take effect until the end of the period of 14 days beginning with the day on which it is given, unless the local authority agree that it is to take effect at the end of a shorter period.

Sunday Trading Act 1994, Sch 1

(4) A notice under this paragraph shall cease to have effect when superseded by a subsequent notice or cancelled as mentioned in sub-paragraph (2)(b) above.

Register of shops

5.—(1) Every local authority shall keep a register of shops in respect of which a notice under paragraph 4 above has effect.

(2) In relation to every such shop, the register shall contain particulars of—
   (a) the name (if any) and address of the shop, and
   (b) the permitted Sunday opening hours specified in the notice under paragraph 4 above.

(3) Any register kept under this paragraph—
   (a) shall be open to inspection by members of the public at all reasonable times, and
   (b) may be kept by means of a computer.

Duty to display notice

6. At any time when—
   (a) a large shop is open on Sunday for the serving of retail customers, and
   (b) the prohibition in sub-paragraph (1) of paragraph 2 above is excluded only by sub-paragraph (3) of that paragraph,

a notice specifying the permitted Sunday opening hours specified in the notice under paragraph 4 above shall be displayed in a conspicuous position inside and outside the shop.

Offences

7.—(1) If paragraph 2(1) above is contravened in relation to a shop, the occupier of the shop shall be liable on summary conviction to a fine not exceeding £50,000.

(2) If paragraph 6 above is contravened in relation to a shop, the occupier of the shop shall be liable on summary conviction to a fine not exceeding level 2 on the standard scale.

8. Where a person is charged with having contravened paragraph 2(1) above, in relation to a large shop which was permitted to be open for the serving of retail customers on the Sunday in question during the permitted Sunday opening hours specified in a notice under paragraph 4 above, by reason of his having served a retail customer after the end of those hours, it shall be a defence to prove that the customer was in the shop before that time and left not later than half an hour after that time.

Transitional provision

9. Any notice given for the purposes of paragraph 4(1) above after the passing of this Act but before the commencement of this Schedule shall, notwithstanding paragraph 4(3) above, take effect on that commencement.

References   See Chapters 4 and 5.

SCHEDULE 2

Section 1(1)

SUPPLEMENTARY PROVISIONS

PART I

GENERAL ENFORCEMENT PROVISIONS

Duty to enforce Act

1. It shall be the duty of every local authority to enforce within their area the provisions of Schedules 1 and 3 to this Act and Part II of this Schedule.

Inspectors

2. For the purposes of their duties under paragraph 1 above it shall be the duty of every local authority to appoint inspectors.

Powers of entry

3. An inspector appointed by a local authority under paragraph 2 above shall, on producing if so required some duly authenticated document showing his authority, have a right at all reasonable hours—
- (a) to enter any premises within the area of the local authority, with or without a constable, for the purpose of ascertaining whether there is or has been on the premises any contravention of the provisions of Schedules 1 and 3 to this Act,
- (b) to require the production of, inspect and take copies of any records (in whatever form they are held) relating to any business carried on on the premises which appear to him to be relevant for the purpose mentioned in paragraph (a) above,
- (c) where those records are kept by means of a computer, to require the records to be produced in a form in which they may be taken away, and
- (d) to take such measurements and photographs as he considers necessary for the purpose mentioned in paragraph (a) above.

Obstruction of inspectors

4. Any person who intentionally obstructs an inspector appointed under paragraph 2 above acting in the execution of his duty shall be liable on summary conviction to a fine not exceeding level 3 on the standard scale.

Offences due to fault of other person

5. Where the commission by any person of an offence under this Act is due to the act or default of some other person, that other person shall be guilty of the offence, and a person may be charged with and convicted of the offence by virtue of this paragraph whether or not proceedings are taken against the first-mentioned person.

Offences by bodies corporate

6.—(1) Where an offence under this Act committed by a body corporate is proved to have been committed with the consent or connivance of, or to be attributable to any neglect on the part of, any director, manager, secretary or other similar officer of the body corporate, or any person who was purporting to act in any such capacity, he as well as the body corporate shall be guilty of the offence and shall be liable to be proceeded against and punished accordingly.

(2) Where the affairs of a body corporate are managed by its members, sub- paragraph (1) above shall apply in relation to the acts and defaults of a member in connection with his functions of management as if he were a director of the body corporate.

Defence of due diligence

7.—(1) In any proceedings for an offence under this Act it shall, subject to sub-paragraph (2) below, be a defence for the person charged to prove that he took all reasonable precautions and exercised all due diligence to avoid the commission of the offence by himself or by a person under his control.

(2) If in any case the defence provided by sub-paragraph (1) above involves the allegation that the commission of the offence was due to the act or default of another person, the person charged shall not, without leave of the court, be entitled to rely on that defence unless, at least seven clear days before the hearing, he has served on the prosecutor a notice in writing giving such information identifying or assisting in the identification of that other person as was then in his possession.

References See Chapters 9 and 10.

PART II

SHOPS OCCUPIED BY PERSONS OBSERVING THE JEWISH SABBATH

Shops occupied by persons of the Jewish religion

8.—(1) A person of the Jewish religion who is the occupier of a large shop may give to the local authority for the area in which the shop is situated a notice signed by him stating—
- (a) that he is a person of the Jewish religion, and

(b) that he intends to keep the shop closed for the serving of customers on the Jewish Sabbath.

(2) For the purposes of this paragraph, a shop occupied by a partnership or company shall be taken to be occupied by a person of the Jewish religion if, and only if, the majority of the partners or of the directors, as the case may be, are persons of that religion.

(3) A notice under sub-paragraph (1) above shall be accompanied by a certificate signed by an authorised person that the person giving the notice is a person of the Jewish religion.

(4) Where the occupier of the shop is a partnership or company—
  (a) any notice under sub-paragraph (1) above shall be given by the majority of the partners or directors and, if not given by all of them, shall specify the names of the other partners or directors, and
  (b) a certificate under sub-paragraph (3) above is required in relation to each of the persons by whom such a notice is given.

(5) Every local authority shall keep a register containing particulars of the name (if any) and address of every shop in respect of which a notice under sub-paragraph (1) above has effect.

(6) Any register kept under this paragraph—
  (a) shall be open to inspection by members of the public at all reasonable times, and
  (b) may be kept by means of a computer.

(7) If there is any change
  (a) in the occupation of a shop in respect of which a notice under sub-paragraph (1) above has effect, or
  (b) in any partnership or among the directors of any company by which such a shop is occupied,

the notice shall be taken to be cancelled at the end of the period of 14 days beginning with the day on which the change occurred, unless during that period, or within such further time as may be allowed by the local authority, a fresh notice is given under sub-paragraph (1) above in respect of the shop.

(8) Where a fresh notice is given under sub-paragraph (1) above by reason of a change of the kind mentioned in sub-paragraph (7) above, the local authority may dispense with the certificate required by sub-paragraph (3) above in the case of any person in respect of whom such a certificate has been provided in connection with a former notice in respect of that shop or any other shop in the area of the local authority.

(9) A notice given under sub-paragraph (1) above in respect of any shop shall be cancelled on application in that behalf being made to the local authority by the occupier of the shop.

(10) A person who, in a notice or certificate given for the purposes of this paragraph, makes a statement which is false in a material respect and which he knows to be false or does not believe to be true shall be liable on summary conviction to a fine not exceeding level 5 on the standard scale.

(11) Where a person is convicted of an offence under sub-paragraph (10) above, the local authority may cancel any notice under sub-paragraph (1) above to which the offence relates.

(12) In this paragraph—
  "authorised person", in relation to a notice under sub-paragraph (1) above, means—
    (a) the Minister of the synagogue of which the person giving the notice is a member,
    (b) the secretary of that synagogue, or
    (c) any other person nominated for the purposes of this paragraph by the President of the London Committee of Deputies of the British Jews (otherwise known as the Board of Deputies of British Jews),
  "large shop" and "shop" have the same meaning as in Schedule 1 to this Act, and
  "secretary of a synagogue" has the same meaning as in Part IV of the Marriage Act 1949.

Members of other religious bodies observing the Jewish Sabbath

9. Paragraph 8 above shall apply to persons who are members of any religious body regularly observing the Jewish Sabbath as it applies to persons of the Jewish religion, and accordingly—

(a) references to persons of the Jewish religion shall be construed as including any person who is a member of such a body, and
(b) in the application of that paragraph to such persons "authorised person" means a Minister of the religious body concerned.

Transitional provisions

10.—(1) Any shop which is registered under section 53 of the Shops Act 1950 at the commencement of this Schedule and is at that time a large shop within the meaning of Schedule 1 to this Act shall be taken to be a shop in respect of which a notice has been given under sub-paragraph (1) of paragraph 8 above by the person who was then registered as the occupier of the shop; and the provisions of that paragraph in relation to the cancellation of such a notice shall have effect accordingly.

(2) In paragraph 8(8) above, the reference to a certificate provided in connection with a former notice includes a reference to a statutory declaration provided under subsection (2) of section 53 of the Shops Act 1950 in connection with the registration of a shop under that section before the commencement of this Schedule.

References   See Chapter 8.

SCHEDULE 3

Section 2

LOADING AND UNLOADING AT LARGE SHOPS ON SUNDAY MORNING

Shops to which Schedule applies

1. This Schedule applies to any shop—
(a) which is a large shop, within the meaning of Schedule 1 to this Act, in respect of which a notice under paragraph 4 of that Schedule has effect, and
(b) which is situated in an area designated as a loading control area under section 2 of this Act.

Consent required for early Sunday loading and unloading

2. The occupier of a shop to which this Schedule applies shall not load or unload, or permit any other person to load or unload, goods from a vehicle at the shop before 9 am. on Sunday in connection with the trade or business carried on in the shop, unless the loading or unloading is carried on—
(a) with the consent of the local authority for the area in which the shop is situated granted under this Schedule, and
(b) in accordance with any conditions subject to which that consent is granted.

3.—(1) A consent under this Schedule may be granted subject to such conditions as the local authority consider appropriate.

(2) The local authority may at any time vary the conditions subject to which a consent is granted, and shall give notice of the variation to the person to whom the consent was granted.

Application for consent

4. An application for a consent under this Schedule shall be made in writing and shall contain such information as the local authority may reasonably require.

5. An applicant for a consent under this Schedule shall pay such reasonable fee in respect of his application as the local authority may determine.

6.—(1) Where an application is duly made to the local authority for a consent under this Schedule, the authority shall grant the consent unless they are satisfied that the loading or unloading of goods from vehicles before 9 am on Sunday at the shop to which the application relates, in connection with the trade or business carried on at the shop, has caused, or would be likely to cause, undue annoyance to local residents.

(2) The authority shall determine the application and notify the applicant in writing of their decision within the period of 21 days beginning with the day on which the application is received by the authority.

(3) In a case where a consent is granted, the notification under sub-paragraph (2) above shall specify the conditions, if any, subject to which the consent is granted.

Revocation of consent

7. Where—
   (a) the occupier of a shop in respect of which a consent under this Schedule is in force is convicted of an offence under paragraph 9 below by reason of his failure to comply with the conditions subject to which the consent was granted, or
   (b) the local authority are satisfied that the loading or unloading authorised by virtue of a consent under this Schedule has caused undue annoyance to local residents,

the local authority may revoke the consent.

Publication of consent

8. Where a local authority grant a consent under this Schedule, the authority may cause a notice giving details of that consent to be published in a local newspaper circulating in their area.

Offence

9. A person who contravenes paragraph 2 above shall be liable on summary conviction to a fine not exceeding level 3 on the standard scale.

References   See Chapter 6.

SCHEDULE 4

Section 4

RIGHTS OF SHOP WORKERS AS RESPECTS SUNDAY WORKING

Interpretation

1.—(1) In this Schedule, except where a contrary intention appears—
"the 1978 Act" means the Employment Protection (Consolidation) Act 1978,
"catering business" means—
   (a) the sale of meals, refreshments or intoxicating liquor for consumption on the premises on which they are sold, or
   (b) the sale of meals or refreshments prepared to order for immediate consumption off the premises,
"the commencement date" means the day on which this Schedule comes into force,
"dismissal" has the same meaning as in Part V of the 1978 Act,
"intoxicating liquor" has the same meaning as in the Licensing Act 1964,
"notice period", in relation to an opting-out notice, has the meaning given by paragraph 6 below,
"opted-out", in relation to a shop worker, shall be construed in accordance with paragraph 5 below,
"opting-in notice" has the meaning given by paragraph 3(2) below,
"opting-out notice" has the meaning given by paragraph 4(3) below,
"protected", in relation to a shop worker, shall be construed in accordance with paragraphs 2 and 3 below,
"retail trade or business" includes—
   (a) the business of a barber or hairdresser,
   (b) the business of hiring goods otherwise than for use in the course of a trade or business, and
   (c) retail sales by auction,
but does not include catering business or the sale at theatres and places of amusement of programmes, catalogues and similar items,
"shop" includes, subject to sub-paragraph (2) below, any premises where any retail trade or business is carried on,
"shop work" means work in or about a shop in England or Wales on a day on which the shop is open for the serving of customers, and
"shop worker" means an employee who, under his contract of employment, is required to do shop work or may be required to do such work.

(2) Where premises are used mainly for purposes other than those of retail trade or business and would not apart from sub-paragraph (1) above be regarded as a shop, only such part of the premises as—
- (a) is used wholly or mainly for the purposes of retail trade or business, or
- (b) is used both for the purposes of retail trade or business and for the purposes of wholesale trade and is used wholly or mainly for those two purposes considered together,

is to be regarded as a shop for the purposes of this Schedule.

(3) In sub-paragraph (2) above "wholesale trade" means the sale of goods for use or resale in the course of a business or the hire of goods for use in the course of a business.

(4) Subject to sub-paragraph (5) below, the following provisions of the 1978 Act—
section 151(1) and (2) (computation of period of continuous employment), and
section 153 (general interpretation),

shall have effect for the purposes of this Schedule as they have effect for the purposes of that Act.

(5) For the purposes of this Schedule, section 151(2) of the 1978 Act shall have effect with the omission of the words from "but" onwards and Schedule 13 to that Act shall have effect with the following modifications—
- (a) in paragraph 1 for the words "paragraphs 3 to 12" there shall be substituted "paragraph 4 or paragraphs 9 to 12",
- (b) paragraph 3 and paragraphs 5 to 8 shall be omitted, and
- (c) in paragraph 4 the words "which normally involves employment for sixteen hours or more weekly" shall be omitted.

(6) Where section 56 of the 1978 Act (failure to permit woman to return to work after childbirth treated as dismissal) applies to an employee who was employed as a shop worker under her contract of employment on the last day of her maternity leave period, she shall be treated for the purposes of this Schedule as if she had been employed as a shop worker on the day with effect from which she is treated as dismissed under that section.

Meaning of "protected shop worker"

2.—(1) Subject to paragraph 3 below, a shop worker is to be regarded for the purposes of this Schedule as "protected" if, and only if, sub-paragraph (2) or (3) below applies to him.

(2) This sub-paragraph applies to a shop worker if—
- (a) on the day before the commencement date, he was employed as a shop worker,
- (b) on that day, he was not employed to work only on Sunday,
- (c) he has been continuously employed during the period beginning with that day and ending with the appropriate date, and
- (d) throughout that period, or throughout every part of it during which his relations with his employer were governed by a contract of employment, he was a shop worker.

(3) This sub-paragraph applies to any shop worker whose contract of employment is such that under it he—
- (a) is not, and may not be, required to work on Sunday, and
- (b) could not be so required even if the provisions of this Schedule were disregarded.

(4) In sub-paragraph (2)(c) above "the appropriate date" means—
- (a) in relation to paragraphs 7 and 8 below, the effective date of termination,
- (b) in relation to paragraph 10 below, the date of the act or failure to act,
- (c) in relation to sub-paragraph (2) or (3) of paragraph 12 below, the day on which the agreement is entered into,
- (d) in relation to sub-paragraph (4) of that paragraph, the day on which the employee returns to work,
- (e) in relation to paragraph 14 below, any time in relation to which the contract is to be enforced, and
- (f) in relation to paragraph 15 below, the end of the period in respect of which the remuneration is paid or the benefit accrues.

(5) For the purposes of sub-paragraph (4)(a) above, "the effective date of termination", in any case falling within paragraph 1(6) above, means the day with effect from which the employee is treated by section 56 of the 1978 Act as being dismissed.

Sunday Trading Act 1994, Sch 4

(6) For the purposes of sub-paragraph (4)(b) above—
 (a) where an act extends over a period, the "date of the act" means the first day of the period, and
 (b) a deliberate failure to act shall be treated as done when it was decided on,

and in the absence of evidence establishing the contrary, an employer shall be taken to decide on a failure to act when he does an act inconsistent with doing the failed act or, if he has done no such inconsistent act, when the period expires within which he might reasonably have been expected to do the failed act if it was to be done.

(7) Where on the day before the commencement date an employee's relations with his employer have ceased to be governed by a contract of employment, he shall be regarded as satisfying the conditions in sub-paragraph (2)(a) and (b) above if—
 (a) that day falls in a week which counts as a period of employment with that employer under paragraph 9 or 10 of Schedule 13 to the 1978 Act (absence from work because of sickness, pregnancy etc) or under regulations made under paragraph 20 of that Schedule (reinstatement or re-engagement of dismissed employee), and
 (b) on the last day before the commencement date on which his relations with his employer were governed by a contract of employment, the employee was a shop worker and was not employed to work only on Sunday.

3.—(1) A shop worker is not a protected shop worker if—
 (a) on or after the commencement date, he has given his employer an opting-in notice, and
 (b) after giving that notice, he has expressly agreed with his employer to do shop work on Sunday or on a particular Sunday.

(2) In this Schedule "opting-in notice" means a written notice, signed and dated by the shop worker, in which the shop worker expressly states that he wishes to work on Sunday or that he does not object to Sunday working.

Notice of objection to Sunday working

4.—(1) This paragraph applies to any shop worker who, under his contract of employment—
 (a) is or may be required to work on Sunday (whether or not as a result of previously giving an opting-in notice), but
 (b) is not employed to work only on Sunday.

(2) A shop worker to whom this paragraph applies may at any time give his employer written notice, signed and dated by the shop worker, to the effect that the shop worker objects to Sunday working.

(3) In this Schedule "opting-out notice" means a notice given under sub-paragraph (2) above by a shop worker to whom this paragraph applies.

Meaning of "opted-out shop worker"

5.—(1) Subject to sub-paragraph (5) below, a shop worker is to be regarded for the purposes of this Schedule as "opted-out" if, and only if—
 (a) he has given his employer an opting-out notice,
 (b) he has been continuously employed during the period beginning with the day on which the notice was given and ending with the appropriate date, and
 (c) throughout that period, or throughout every part of it during which his relations with his employer were governed by a contract of employment, he was a shop worker.

(2) In sub-paragraph (1) above "the appropriate date" means—
 (a) in relation to paragraphs 7 and 8 below, the effective date of termination,
 (b) in relation to paragraph 10 below, the date of the act or failure to act,
 (c) in relation to sub-paragraph (2) or (3) of paragraph 13 below, the day on which the agreement is entered into, and
 (d) in relation to sub-paragraph (4) of that paragraph, the day on which the employee returns to work.

(3) For the purposes of sub-paragraph (2)(a) above, "the effective date of termination", in any case falling within paragraph 1(6) above, means the day with effect from which the employee is treated by section 56 of the 1978 Act as being dismissed.

Sunday Trading Act 1994, Sch 4

(4) For the purposes of sub-paragraph (2)(b) above—
  (a) where an act extends over a period, the "date of the act" means the first day of the period, and
  (b) a deliberate failure to act shall be treated as done when it was decided on,

and in the absence of evidence establishing the contrary, an employer shall be taken to decide on a failure to act when he does an act inconsistent with doing the failed act or, if he has done no such inconsistent act, when the period expires within which he might reasonably have been expected to do the failed act if it was to be done.

(5) A shop worker is not an opted-out shop worker if—
  (a) after giving the opting-out notice concerned, he has given his employer an opting-in notice, and
  (b) after giving that opting-in notice, he has expressly agreed with his employer to do shop work on Sunday or on a particular Sunday.

Meaning of "notice period"

6. In this Schedule "notice period", in relation to an opted-out shop worker, means, subject to paragraph 11(2) below, the period of three months beginning with the day on which the opting-out notice concerned was given.

Right not to be dismissed for refusing Sunday work

7.—(1) Subject to sub-paragraph (2) below, the dismissal of a protected or opted-out shop worker by his employer shall be regarded for the purposes of Part V of the 1978 Act as unfair if the reason for it (or, if more than one, the principal reason) was that the shop worker refused, or proposed to refuse, to do shop work on Sunday or on a particular Sunday.

(2) Sub-paragraph (1) above does not apply in relation to an opted-out shop worker where the reason (or principal reason) for the dismissal was that he refused, or proposed to refuse, to do shop work on any Sunday or Sundays falling before the end of the notice period.

(3) The dismissal of a shop worker by his employer shall be regarded for the purposes of Part V of the 1978 Act as unfair if the reason for it (or, if more than one, the principal reason) was that the shop worker gave, or proposed to give, an opting-out notice to the employer.

(4) Section 142 of the 1978 Act (contracts for a fixed term) shall not exclude the application of section 54 of that Act (right of employee not to be unfairly dismissed) in relation to any dismissal which is unfair by virtue of sub-paragraph (1) or (3) above.

8.—(1) Where the reason or principal reason for the dismissal of a protected or opted-out shop worker was that he was redundant, but it is shown—
  (a) that the circumstances constituting the redundancy applied equally to one or more other employees in the same undertaking who held positions similar to that held by him and who have not been dismissed by the employer, and
  (b) that the reason (or, if more than one, the principal reason) for which he was selected for dismissal was that specified in paragraph 7(1) above,

then, for the purposes of Part V of the 1978 Act, the dismissal shall be regarded as unfair.

(2) Sub-paragraph (1) above does not apply in relation to an opted-out shop worker where the reason (or principal reason) for which he was selected for dismissal was that specified in paragraph 7(2) above.

(3) Where the reason or principal reason for the dismissal of a shop worker was that he was redundant, but it is shown—
  (a) that the circumstances constituting the redundancy applied equally to one or more other employees in the same undertaking who held positions similar to that held by him and who have not been dismissed by the employer, and
  (b) that the reason (or, if more than one, the principal reason) for which he was selected for dismissal was that specified in paragraph 7(3) above,

then, for the purposes of Part V of the 1978 Act, the dismissal shall be regarded as unfair.

Exclusion of section 64(1) of Employment Protection (Consolidation) Act 1978

9. Section 54 of the 1978 Act (right of employee not to be unfairly dismissed) shall apply to a dismissal regarded as unfair by virtue of paragraph 7 or 8 above regardless of the period for

Sunday Trading Act 1994, Sch 4

which the employee has been employed and of his age; and accordingly section 64(1) of that Act (which provides a qualifying period and an upper age limit) shall not apply to such a dismissal.

Right not to suffer detriment for refusing Sunday work

10.—(1) Subject to sub-paragraphs (2) and (4) below, a protected or opted-out shop worker has the right not to be subjected to any detriment by any act, or any deliberate failure to act, by his employer done on the ground that the shop worker refused, or proposed to refuse, to do shop work on Sunday or on a particular Sunday.

(2) Sub-paragraph (1) above does not apply to anything done in relation to an opted-out shop worker on the ground that he refused, or proposed to refuse, to do shop work on any Sunday or Sundays falling before the end of the notice period.

(3) Subject to sub-paragraph (4) below, a shop worker has the right not to be subjected to any detriment by any act, or any deliberate failure to act, by his employer done on the ground that he gave, or proposed to give, an opting-out notice to his employer.

(4) Sub-paragraphs (1) and (3) above do not apply where the detriment in question amounts to dismissal.

(5) For the purposes of this paragraph a shop worker who does not work on Sunday or on a particular Sunday is not to be regarded as having been subjected to any detriment by—
  (a) any failure to pay remuneration in respect of shop work on a Sunday which he has not done,
  (b) any failure to provide him with any other benefit, where that failure results from the application, in relation to a Sunday on which the employee has not done shop work, of a contractual term under which the extent of that benefit varies according to the number of hours worked by the employee or the remuneration of the employee, or
  (c) any failure to provide him with any work, remuneration or other benefit which by virtue of paragraph 14 or 15 below the employer is not obliged to provide.

(6) Where an employer offers to pay a sum specified in the offer to any one or more employees who are protected or opted-out shop workers or who, under their contracts of employment, are not obliged to do shop work on Sunday, if they agree to do shop work on Sunday or on a particular Sunday—
  (a) an employee to whom the offer is not made is not to be regarded for the purposes of this paragraph as having been subjected to any detriment by any failure to make the offer to him or to pay him that sum, and
  (b) an employee who does not accept the offer is not to be regarded for those purposes as having been subjected to any detriment by any failure to pay him that sum.

Employer's duty to give explanatory statement

11.—(1) Where a person becomes a shop worker to whom paragraph 4 above applies, his employer shall, before the end of the period of two months beginning with the day on which that person becomes such a shop worker, give him a written statement in the prescribed form.

(2) If—
  (a) an employer fails to comply with sub-paragraph (1) above in relation to any shop worker, and
  (b) the shop worker, on giving the employer an opting-out notice, becomes an opted-out shop worker,

paragraph 6 above shall have effect, in relation to the shop worker, with the substitution for "three months" of "one month".

(3) An employer shall not be regarded as failing to comply with sub-paragraph (1) above in any case where, before the end of the period referred to in that sub-paragraph, the shop worker has given him an opting-out notice.

(4) Subject to sub-paragraph (5) below, the prescribed form is as follows—

"STATUTORY RIGHTS IN RELATION TO SUNDAY SHOP WORK

You have become employed as a shop worker and are or can be required under your contract of employment to do the Sunday work your contract provides for.

However, if you wish, you can give a notice, as described in the next paragraph, to your employer and you will then have the right not to work in or about a shop on any Sunday on which the shop is open once three months have passed from the date on which you gave the notice.

Your notice must—

be in writing;

be signed and dated by you;

say that you object to Sunday working.

For three months after you give the notice, your employer can still require you to do all the Sunday work your contract provides for. After the three month period has ended, you have the right to complain to an industrial tribunal if, because of your refusal to work on Sundays on which the shop is open, your employer—

dismisses you, or

does something else detrimental to you, for example, failing to promote you.

Once you have the rights described, you can surrender them only by giving your employer a further notice, signed and dated by you, saying that you wish to work on Sunday or that you do not object to Sunday-working and then agreeing with your employer to work on Sundays or on a particular Sunday.".

(5) The Secretary of State may by order amend the prescribed form set out in sub-paragraph (4) above.

(6) An order under sub-paragraph (5) above shall be made by statutory instrument which shall be subject to annulment in pursuance of a resolution of either House of Parliament.

Effect of rights on contracts of employment

12.—(1) Any contract of employment under which a shop worker who satisfies the conditions in paragraph 2(2)(a) and (b) above was employed on the day before the commencement date is unenforceable to the extent that it—

(a) requires the shop worker to do shop work on Sunday on or after the commencement date, or

(b) requires the employer to provide the shop worker with shop work on Sunday on or after that date.

(2) Except as provided by sub-paragraph (3) below, any agreement entered into after the commencement date between a protected shop worker and his employer is unenforceable to the extent that it—

(a) requires the shop worker to do shop work on Sunday, or

(b) requires the employer to provide the shop worker with shop work on Sunday.

(3) Where, after giving an opting-in notice, a protected shop worker expressly agrees as mentioned in paragraph 3(1)(b) above (and so ceases to be protected), his contract of employment shall be taken to be varied to the extent necessary to give effect to the terms of the agreement.

(4) The reference in sub-paragraph (2) above to a protected shop worker includes a reference to an employee who, although not a protected shop worker for the purposes of that sub-paragraph at the time when the agreement is entered into, is a protected shop worker on the day on which she returns to work as mentioned in paragraph 10 of Schedule 13 to the 1978 Act (maternity).

13.—(1) Where a shop worker gives his employer an opting-out notice, the contract of employment under which he was employed immediately before he gave that notice becomes unenforceable to the extent that it—

(a) requires the shop worker to do shop work on Sunday after the end of the notice period, or

(b) requires the employer to provide the shop worker with shop work on Sunday after the end of that period.

(2) Except as provided by sub-paragraph (3) below, any agreement entered into between an opted-out shop worker and his employer is unenforceable to the extent that it—

(a) requires the shop worker to do shop work on Sunday after the end of the notice period, or

(b) requires the employer to provide the shop worker with shop work on Sunday after the end of that period.

(3) Where, after giving an opting-in notice, an opted-out shop worker expressly agrees as mentioned in paragraph 5(5)(b) above (and so ceases to be opted-out), his contract of employment shall be taken to be varied to the extent necessary to give effect to the terms of the agreement.

(4) The reference in sub-paragraph (2) above to an opted-out shop worker includes a reference to an employee who, although not an opted-out shop worker for the purposes of that sub-paragraph at the time when the agreement is entered into, had given her employer an opting-out notice before that time and is an opted-out shop worker on the day on which she returns to work as mentioned in paragraph 10 of Schedule 13 to the 1978 Act (maternity).

14. If—
   (a) under the contract of employment under which a shop worker who satisfies the conditions in paragraph 2(2)(a) and (b) above was employed on the day before the commencement date, the employer is, or may be, required to provide him with shop work for a specified number of hours each week,
   (b) under that contract, the shop worker was or might have been required to work on Sunday before the commencement date, and
   (c) the shop worker has done shop work on Sunday in that employment (whether or not before the commencement date) but has, on or after the commencement date, ceased to do so,

then, so long as the shop worker remains a protected shop worker, that contract shall not be regarded as requiring the employer to provide him with shop work on weekdays in excess of the hours normally worked by the shop worker on weekdays before he ceased to do shop work on Sunday.

15.—(1) If—
   (a) under the contract of employment under which a shop worker who satisfies the conditions in paragraph 2(2)(a) and (b) above was employed on the day before the commencement date, the shop worker was or might have been required to work on Sunday before that date,
   (b) the shop worker has done shop work on Sunday in that employment (whether or not before the commencement date) but has, on or after the commencement date, ceased to do so, and
   (c) it is not apparent from the contract what part of the remuneration payable, or of any other benefit accruing, to the shop worker was intended to be attributable to shop work on Sunday,

then, so long as the shop worker remains a protected shop worker, that contract shall be regarded as enabling the employer to reduce the amount of remuneration paid, or the extent of the other benefit provided, to the shop worker in respect of any period by the proportion which the hours of shop work which (apart from this Schedule) the shop worker could have been required to do on Sunday in the period (in this paragraph referred to as "the contractual Sunday hours") bears to the aggregate of those hours and the hours of work actually done by the shop worker in the period.

(2) Where, under the contract of employment, the hours of work actually done on weekdays in any period would be taken into account in determining the contractual Sunday hours, they shall be taken into account in determining the contractual Sunday hours for the purposes of sub-paragraph (1) above.

Proceedings for contravention of paragraph 10

16. Sections 22B and 22C of the 1978 Act (which relate to proceedings brought by an employee on the ground that he has been subjected to a detriment in contravention of section 22A of that Act) shall have effect as if the reference in section 22B(1) to section 22A included a reference to paragraph 10 above.

Restrictions on contracting out of Schedule

17.—(1) Any provision in an agreement (whether a contract of employment or not) shall be void in so far as it purports—
   (a) to exclude or limit the operation of any provision of this Schedule, or
   (b) to preclude any person from presenting a complaint to an industrial tribunal by virtue of any provision of this Schedule.

(2) Sub-paragraph (1) above does not apply to an agreement to refrain from presenting or continuing with a complaint where—
  (a) a conciliation officer has taken action under section 133(2) or (3) of the 1978 Act (general provisions as to conciliation) or under section 134(1), (2) or (3) (conciliation in case of unfair dismissal) of that Act, or
  (b) the conditions regulating compromise agreements under the 1978 Act (as set out in section 140(3) of that Act) are satisfied in relation to the agreement.

Transitional modifications relating to maternity cases

18.—(1) Where an employee exercises a right to return to work under Part III of the 1978 Act (maternity) and, because amendments of that Part made by the Trade Union Reform and Employment Rights Act 1993 (in this paragraph referred to as "the 1993 Act") do not have effect in her case, her right is a right to return to work in the job in which she was employed under the original contract of employment—
  (a) the preceding provisions of this Schedule shall have effect subject to the modifications in sub-paragraphs (2) and (3) below, and
  (b) sub-paragraph (4) below shall have effect.

(2) In paragraph 1(6), for "her contract of employment on the last day of her maternity leave period" there shall be substituted "her original contract of employment".

(3) In paragraph 2(7), for paragraph (b) there shall be substituted—
  "(b) under her original contract of employment, she was a shopworker and was not employed to work only on Sunday".

(4) If the employee was employed as a shop worker under her original contract of employment, she shall not be regarded as failing to satisfy the condition in paragraph 2(2)(a) or (d) or 5(1)(c) above merely because during her pregnancy she was employed under a different contract of employment by virtue of section 60(2) of the 1978 Act (as it has effect before the commencement of section 24 of the 1993 Act) or otherwise by reason of her pregnancy.

(5) In this paragraph and in paragraphs 1 and 2 above as modified by sub-paragraphs (2) and (3) above "original contract of employment" has the meaning given by section 153(1) of the 1978 Act as originally enacted.

Dismissal on grounds of assertion of statutory right

19. In section 60A of the 1978 Act (dismissal on grounds of assertion of statutory right), in subsection (4)(a), after sub-paragraph (ii) there shall be inserted "or
  (iii) Schedule 4 to the Sunday Trading Act 1994".

Dismissal procedures agreements

20. In section 65 of the 1978 Act (exclusion in respect of dismissal procedures agreement) at the end of subsection (4) there shall be added "or the right conferred by paragraph 7 or 8 of Schedule 4 to the Sunday Trading Act 1994".

Conciliation

21. In section 133 of the 1978 Act (general provisions as to conciliation officers) at the end of subsection (1) there shall be added—
  "(ee) arising out of a contravention, or alleged contravention, of paragraph 10 of Schedule 4 to the Sunday Trading Act 1994."

Application of certain other provisions of 1978 Act

22. In the following provisions of the 1978 Act—
  section 129 (remedy for infringement of certain rights),
  section 141(2) (employee ordinarily working outside Great Britain), and
  section 150 and Schedule 12 (death of employee or employer),
any reference to Part II of the 1978 Act includes a reference to paragraph 10 of this Schedule.

Keeping of records relating to Sunday employment

23. In section 22 of the Shops Act 1950 (Sunday employment), in subsection (3) (keeping of records) for "by virtue of any provision of Part IV of this Act, other than section sixty-two, is" there shall be substituted "is lawfully".

Sunday Trading Act 1994, Sch 4

Employment of children in street trading on Sunday

24. In section 20 of the Children and Young Persons Act 1933, subsection (3) (which provides that byelaws under that section may not authorise a child to engage, or be employed, on a Sunday in street trading of a description to which certain provisions of Part IV of the Shops Act 1950 do not apply) shall cease to have effect.

References   See Chapters 11 and 12.

SCHEDULE 5

Section 9(2)

REPEALS

Chapter	Short title	Extent of repeal
1933 c 12	The Children and Young Persons Act 1933	Section 20(3)
1950 c 28	The Shops Act 1950	Sections 47 to 66 In section 71(7)(b), the words "or Part IV" Schedules 5, 6 and 7
1962 c 35	The Shops (Airports) Act 1962	In section 1(1) the words from "and of" to "Sunday trading)"
1963 c 33	The London Government Act 1963	Section 51(3)
1963 c 37	The Children and Young Persons Act 1963	Section 35(3)
1965 c 35	The Shops (Early Closing Days) Act 1965	In section 4(2), the words from "and notwithstanding" to the end
1969 c 48	The Post Office Act 1969	In Schedule 4, in paragraph 51, the words from "and Schedule 5" to "on Sunday)"
1986 c 31	The Airports Act 1986	Section 70 In Schedule 5, paragraph 15
1989 c 38	The Employment Act 1989	In Schedule 3, in Part III, paragraph 2(c)

Appendix 2

Precedents

Precedent 1

Notice of Proposed Sunday Opening

NOTICE OF PROPOSED SUNDAY OPENING pursuant to Sch 1 para 4(1) of the Sunday Trading Act 1994.

NAME OF OCCUPIER

ADDRESS OF OCCUPIER FOR CORRESPONDENCE IN RESPECT OF THIS NOTICE

NAME (IF ANY) AND ADDRESS OF THE SHOP TO WHICH THIS NOTICE RELATES

I/WE hereby give you notice that the above occupier intends to open the above shop on Sundays for the retail service of customers. The permitted Sunday opening hours shall be   am to   pm.

DATED [   ]

SIGNED ....

by and/or on behalf of [the occupier]

Precedent 2

Notice under Schedule 2
Sunday Trading Act 1994

Shops occupied by persons observing the Jewish religion.

**NAME AND ADDRESS OF SHOP TO
WHICH THIS NOTICE APPLIES:**

**NAME AND ADDRESS (ADDRESSES)
OF PERSON(S) GIVING THIS NOTICE:**

**NAME AND ADDRESS OF OCCUPIER
OF SHOP (IF DIFFERENT FROM PERSON
GIVING THIS NOTICE):**

I/We hereby give notice that I am/we are a person(s) of the Jewish Religion and that I/we intend to keep the above shop closed for the serving of customers on Sundays

[If appropriate]

Our fellow partners/directors [delete as appropriate] who do not give this notice are as follows:

NAME   **ADDRESS**

DATED

SIGNED....................
[By each partner giving the notice]
N.B.

1. This application is to be accompanied by a certificate(s) signed by an authorised person confirming that the person(s) giving this notice is/are a person(s) of the Jewish religion

Precedent 3

Notice to Opt-in

1. I hereby give you notice that I do not object to working on Sundays.

2. I have received a copy of a written statement of my statutory rights in relation to Sunday shop work. *[It may be advisable to print the prescribed statutory form on the reverse of this notice.]*

Dated: ....

Signed: ....

Precedent 4

Notice to opt-out

I hereby give you notice that with effect from three months from the date of this notice I am not willing to work on Sundays.

Date: ....

Signed: ....

NOTE:

1. I realise that upon this notice taking effect I will not be entitled to receive any premium or enhanced pay that I currently receive by reason of my working on Sundays.

2. [If applicable] I understand that [the Company] will seek to find me other hours during the week to replace the hours I am at present obliged by my contract to work on Sundays. However, I understand that the company has no statutory obligation to do so and that the replacement hours may not be available.

Precedent 5

Prescribed form describing Statutory Rights in Relation to Sunday Shop Work

You have become employed as a shop worker and are or can be required under your contract of employment to do the Sunday work your contract provides for.

However, if you wish, you can give a notice, as described in the next paragraph, to your employer and you will then have the right not to work in or about a shop on any Sunday on which the shop is open once three months have passed from the date on which you gave the notice.

Your notice must—

be in writing;

be signed and dated by you;

say that you object to Sunday working.

For three months after you give the notice, your employer can still require you to do all the Sunday work your contract provides for. After the three month period has ended, you have the right to complain to an industrial tribunal if, because of your refusal to work on Sundays on which the shop is open, your employer—

dismisses you, or

does something else detrimental to you, for example, failing to promote you.

Once you have the rights described, you can surrender them only by giving your employer a further notice, signed and dated by you, saying that you wish to work on Sunday or that you do not object to Sunday-working and then agreeing with your employer to work on Sundays or on a particular Sunday.

Precedent 6

Shops (Sunday Trading Restrictions) Act 1936

Record of Sunday Employment and of Holidays in Respect of Such Employment

Name of Occupier: **Address of Shop [or place]**

Record for the month of   19 .

Sunday [insert date]

Name of Employed Person	Hour of Commencing Work	Interval for Meals and Rest (if any)	Hour of Ceasing Work	Date of Compensatory Holiday

The four preceding columns to be repeated for each Sunday in the month.

....

[Signed]

[Occupier or Manager]

Index

Airport shop
amendment of provisions relating to, 13.8
designated airport, at, meaning, 5.16
exemption from restrictions, 5.14–5.17
suppliers to, exemption from restrictions, 5.22
Arbitration and Conciliation Advisory Service (ACAS)
resolution of disputes by, 11.76
Art gallery
employment protection provisions –
generally, 11.21
gift shop worker, 11.21
Auction rooms
determining size of, where sale and storage areas combined exceed limits, 2.67
employment protection, 11.15
occasional auctions in hotels etc, exemption from restrictions, 2.25, 2.68
shop, whether constituting, 2.68
Auld Committee
recommendations, 1.10
report, 1.10

Bank
shop, whether constituting, 2.63
Barber
Scotland, regulation of business in, 13.7
Book shops
tabling of amendments to exempt, 1.32
Breach of covenant
Monday to Saturday opening covenant, 7.9
refusal to trade in breach of keep open clause, 7.8, 7.10
Break period
catering staff, 12.24
entitlement to, 12.21–12.25
family shops, 12.22
generally, 12.21–12.25
head office workers, 12.24
managerial staff in stores, 12.24
meals, for, 12.22

Break period – *conitnued*
nature of the entitlement, 12.24
office workers, 12.24
shop assistant's entitlement to –
generally, 12.22, 12.24
shop assistant, meaning, 12.23
transport workers, 12.24
warehouse workers, 12.24
Building society
shop, whether constituting, 2.63
Business name
duty to affix outside place of business, 10.29

Café
exemption from restrictions, 5.4, 5.7
in-store, opening outside six-hour period, letter of explanation with notice, 4.31
large shop, within, whether subject to restrictions, 2.66, 4.20, 4.21
shop, whether constituting, 2.63, 5.7
workers in, exclusion from employment protection provisions, 11.18
Car boot sale
building, operating from inside, 2.62
exemption from legislative changes, 2.25
indoors, whether constituting a shop, 2.64
outdoors, whether constituting a shop, 2.63
shop, whether constituting, 2.57, 2.63, 2.64
Carpet store
explanatory leaflets, provision of, whether a breach of restrictions, 4.7–4.8
Cars. *See* MOTOR TRADE
Cash and carry
employment protection provisions, applicability, 11.20, 11.22
purchasers buying for own use, 2.50
shop, whether constituting, 2.46, 2.64
trading restrictions, 2.46
Catalogue club,
shop, whether constituting, 2.64

121

Index

Catering establishment
  break periods, staff entitlement to, 12.24
  catering business, meaning, 11.17
  generally. *See* CAFÉ; RESTAURANT
  large shop, in, need to exclude customers from rest of shop, 4.21
  meals, refreshments and intoxicating liquor, sale of, 4.20, 4.21
  six-hour period, opening outside, within large shop, 4.21
  workers in, exclusion from employment protection provisions, 11.16–11.19
Chemist shop. *See* PHARMACY
Children
  street trading, repeal of provisions relating to, 13.4, 13.8
Christmas Day
  large shop opening on, 4.18
Church
  employment protection provisions –
    generally, 11.21
    gift shop worker, 11.21
Company
  name, duty to affix outside place of business, 10.29
  occupier, as, 10.28, 10.29
  offence by. *See* DIRECTORS – prosecution of
  prosecution of officers. *See* DIRECTORS – prosecution of
Contract for services
  absence of protection, 11.90
Contract of employment
  extra hours of work on weekdays, provisions as to, 11.86
  maternity leave, protection under, following return from, 11.83
  opting-in notice, effect of giving, 11.83
  opting-out notice, effect of giving, 11.84
  protected worker, position while employee is, 11.86
  rates of pay when ceasing to do Sunday work, provisions as to, 11.86
  SHRC/USDAW undertakings as to, 11.88
  Sunday working, obligations as to, 11.82–11.86
  unenforceable, where, 11.82, 11.84
  variation following opting-in notice, 11.83
  variation following opting-out notice, 11.85
Costco
  judicial review, failure of application in respect to, 2.23

Costco – *continued*
  membership of, 2.22
  retail operation or club, whether constituting, 2.22
County court
  injunction application in, 10.54
  jurisdiction, 10.54
Customers
  serving of. *See* SERVING OF CUSTOMERS
Declaratory judgment
  advisability of court refusing to give, 10.45
Defences
  due diligence –
    acts or omissions by employees, whether large shops can rely on for, 10.69, 10.70
    case law, lack of, 10.65
    generally, 2.52, 3.16
    importance of, in terms of fairness, 10.68
    junior member of staff acting without authority, where, 10.67
    likely areas for application of, 10.66, 10.67
    manager failing to supervise young employee, leading to breach of restrictions, 10.70
    notice destroyed or removed, where, 10.67
    notice of use of defence, need to give, 10.73
    positive action by retailer, need for, 10.69
    problems in demonstrating, 2.52
    statutory nature of, 10.64
    steps to be taken to successfully employ defence, 10.71–10.73
    system to ensure compliance with the law, need to show existence of, 10.72
    vandalism resulting in breach, where, 10.67
  European defences, 10.74–10.79
  generally, 5.11, 10.62
  records, advisability of keeping, 5.11
  shopping up time –
    exclusion, $10.63n^2$
    generally, 10.63
    previous case law, reference to, 10.63
Deregulation and Contracting Out Bill
  generally, 13.1
  proposed repeals under, 13.5–13.7
  Shops Act 1950, s 22, and, 12.4

Index

Designation area
loading etc. *See* LOADING AND
UNLOADING – loading control area

Detriment
employee's right not to suffer. *See*
EMPLOYMENT PROTECTION –
detriment, employee's right not to
suffer

Directors. *See also* MANAGER
aiding and abetting etc the commission of
an offence, 10.24
prosecution of –
acts and defaults of members of
company, for, 10.19
body corporate, following commission
of offence by, 10.18
difficulties under earlier legislation,
10.18
following successful prosecution of
occupier, 10.23
generally, 10.26
senior management aware of breach,
prosecution using powers to
prove, 10.20

Dismissal of employee
protection against, 11.44–11.47 *See also*
EMPLOYMENT PROTECTION
refusal to work on a Sunday falling before
end of notice period, for, 11.45
statutory right, on grounds of assertion of,
11.68
unfair dismissal. *See* UNFAIR DISMISSAL

DIY store
motor accessories, whether certain items
comprising, 1.7
opening for more than six hours –
builder buying paint to paint own
house, 2.51
goods purchased in order to resell, 2.51
restricting sales to non-retail customers,
2.51
regulatory scheme proposals, 1.23
restricting sales to non-retail customers
outside six-hour period, 2.51
restrictions on trading, 5.34
retailer acting as wholeseller, 2.21
tabling of amendments to exempt, 1.32

Dry cleaner
shop, whether constituting, 2.16, 2.63,
5.1

Easter Day
large shop opening on, 4.18

Employment protection
ACAS, resolution of disputes by, 11.76
additional hours of work following refusal
to work on Sunday, whether
employee entitled to, 11.54–11.56
agreement to working on Sundays, effect
of employee giving, 11.37
appropriate date, meaning, 11.26,
11.30–11.32
break periods. *See* BREAK PERIOD
cash and carry, workers in, 11.20, 11.22
catering business –
employees in, exclusion from, 11.16,
11.17–11.19
within store, employees in, 11.9
cleaning or maintenance staff, 11.9
compellable workers, 11.29
conditions –
appropriate date, meaning,
11.30–11.33
dismissed employees, reinstatement or
re-engagement, 11.36
effect, 11.29
employee treated as satisfying,
11.34–11.36
generally, 11.26–11.27
period of employment, as to,
11.34–11.36
contract of employment. *See* CONTRACT
OF EMPLOYMENT
contracting-out, restrictions on –
generally, 11.73
industrial tribunal, as to jurisdiction of,
11.74
industrial tribunal, right to apply to,
11.73
death of employee or employer, 11.77
defects in protection given, 11.89–11.90
delivery drivers, 11.9
detriment, employee's right not to
suffer –
detriment, meaning, 11.51
dismissal, amounting to, 11.52
exclusions for certain potentially
detrimental acts, 11.53
generally, 11.51
industrial tribunal, complaint to. *See*
INDUSTRIAL TRIBUNAL –
complaint to
opted-out worker offered no extra sum
to work on Sundays, 11.61,
11.62
opting-out notice, after giving or
proposing to give, 11.51

123

Index

Employment protection – *continued*
detriment, employee's right not to suffer – *continued*
protected worker offered no extra sum to work on Sundays, 11.61, 11.62
remedies. *See* INDUSTRIAL TRIBUNAL – complaint to
statutory provisions, 11.77
dismissal. *See also* DISMISSAL OF EMPLOYEE; UNFAIR DISMISSAL
protection from, 11.44–11.46
re-employment and, either side of commencement date, effect, 11.89
disputes, resolution by ACAS, 11.76
England and Wales, in, 11.8
exclusions from, 11.10, 11.16, 11.89–11.90
existing protection –
break periods. *See* BREAK PERIOD
constructive dismissal, 12.2, 12.6
criminal liabilities, imposition of, 12.5, 12.6
excessive hours, being forced to work, 12.2
exclusions from protection under, 12.5
four hours, person employed for more than, 12.5, 12.12
generally, 12.1–12.25
holidays, right to, 12.5, 12.7, 12.17–12.19
less than four hours, worker employed for, 12.5
less than two years' continuous employment, worker with, 12.1
limit on number of Sundays to be worked, 12.5, 12.7
no reward, person working for, 12.5
part-time staff, 12.12, 12.13
records, employer's duty to keep. *See* RECORDS – employer's duty to keep
Shops Act, s 22, under, 12.3, 12.5
Sunday-only staff, 12.13
existing shop workers, 11.28
explanatory statement, employer's duty to give –
amendment of prescribed form, 11.81
exemption from duty, 11.81
failure to give, remedy for, 11.80
language of employee, whether to be provided in, 11.81
opting-out notice, effect of employee giving, 11.81

Employment protection – *continued*
explanatory statement, employer's duty to give – *continued*
prescribed form, 11.81
statutory nature of duty, 11.78
time limits for giving, 11.78
to whom notice must be given, 11.78, 11.79
extent of protection, 11.4
generally, 11.1–11.4
loss of protection, 11.37
maternity leave, right to return to work following, 11.75
maximum working hours provisions, defeat of, 11.3
nature of protection, 11.44–11.49
non-compellable workers, 11.29
opting-in notice. *See* OPTING-IN NOTICE
opting-out notice. *See* OPTING-OUT NOTICE
pre-entry discrimination provisions, defeat of, 11.3
premium element under existing contract for working on Sundays, safeguarding, 11.57–11.60
premium pay provisions, defeat of, 11.3
proposals for, 11.1, 11.2
records to be kept. *See* RECORDS
redundant shop workers, 11.47–11.49
retail club, workers in, 11.20, 11.22
services, employment under contract for, 11.90
shop, need to work in, 11.12
shop work, meaning, 11.7
shop worker –
meaning –
question of fact, as, 11.11
statutory definition, 11.6
SHRC/USDAW undertakings –
communication of shop worker rights, as to, 11.88
contract of employment, as to, 11.88
generally, 11.87
lost working hours, as to, 11.88
opting-out notice, as to, 11.88
premium pay, as to, 11.88
standard working week, as to, 11.88
statutory rights, form prescribing, Appendix 2
store management staff, 11.9
system for giving –
conditions to be complied with. *See* conditions *above*
generally, 11.24
types of shop worker, 11.25

Index

Employment protection – *continued*
time off in lieu, entitlement to, 12.5, 12.6, 12.7, 12.13, 12.17–12.20 *See also* HOLIDAY
UK, employment outside, 11.77
voluntary nature of Sunday working, 11.3
warehouse workers attached to stores, 11.9
who are protected, 11.5–11.23
wholesalers, workers in, 11.20, 11.22

Enforcement
injunction, by. *See* INJUNCTION
local authority, duties of. *See* LOCAL AUTHORITY – enforcement duties
magistrates' court, in the –
generally, 10.35–10.41
private citizen's right to prosecute, consideration of, 10.36–10.41
who may prosecute, 10.36–10.41

Estate agents
employment protection, whether entitled to, 11.15
retail trade or business, whether constituting, 2.2
shop, whether constituting, 2.30, 2.63, 5.1

European Court of Justice
reference to –
European courts, by, 1.13
UK courts, by, 1.11, 1.12

Exempt shop
airport shop, 5.14–5.17
chemists, 5.12–5.13
examples, 5.4
exhibition stands, 5.33
failed exemptions, 5.34
generally, 5.1–5.3
hire shop, exemption from restrictions, 5.36–5.40
large farm shops, 5.30–5.32
motor accessory shop, 5.25–5.29
nature of weekday trade, reference to, 5.35
out of town stores in non-food sector, exemption from restrictions, 5.29
petrol filling station –
exemption from restrictions, 5.19–5.21
supermarket, as part of , 5.20, 5.21
pharmacy, 5.12–5.13
ports and harbours, at, 5.22–5.24
purpose of exemptions, 5.3
railway station, at, 5.18
service area –
meaning, 5.19n[1]
exemption for, 5.19

Exempt shop – *continued*
service sector shops, 5.1
video hire shop, 5.36–5.40

Exhibition stands
meaning, 5.33
exemption from restrictions, 5.33

Farm shops
exemption for large farm shops, 5.30–5.32
relevance of nature of weekday trade, 5.35
tabling of amendments to exempt, 1.32

Fines
non-compliance, for, 1.29, 10.4

Foodstuffs
meals or refreshments –
'newly cooked provisions', 1.7
what constitutes, 1.7
whether comprising, 1.7

Garage. *See* MOTOR TRADE

Garden centres
regulatory scheme proposals, 1.23
restrictions on trading, 5.34
tabling of amendments to exempt, 1.32

Gift shop
church, museum, art gallery or similar establishment, employment protection provisions, 11.20, 11.22

Gowers Committee Report
failure of attempt to reform law following, 1.9
findings of, 1.9

Hair salon
employment protection, 11.15
opening in breach of restrictions, shopping up time, defence of, 10.63n[2]
Scotland, regulation of hairdressers' business in, 13.7

Half-holiday
meaning, 12.5

Harbour
shop at, exemption from restrictions, 5.22–5.24

Hire shop
business, whether constituting, within meaning of Shops Acts, 2.9
employment protection, 11.15
exemption from restrictions, 5.36–5.40
former Sunday trading restrictions, whether subject to, 2.7, 2.8, 2.9, 2.10

Index

Hire shop – *continued*
  opening in connection with exemptions, whether need for notice to be given, 5.39
  part of a large shop, where, 5.36
  retail trade or business, whether constituting, 2.2
  shop, whether constituting, 2.63

Holiday
  half-holiday, meaning, 12.5
  right to, under existing legislation, in lieu of Sunday working, 12.5, 12.7, 12.17–12.19
  statutory half-holiday, meaning, 12.5
  voluntarily giving up right to, whether possible, 12.18, 12.19
  whole holiday, meaning, 12.5

Holiday park
  shop within, trading restrictions, 5.34

Holiday resort
  sale of goods at, repeal of provisions relating to, 13.2

Hotel
  occasional auctions/sales on premises, whether subject to restrictions, 2.25, 2.68
  workers in, exclusion from employment protection provisions, 11.18

Industrial tribunal
  complaint to –
    burden of proof, 11.70, 11.71
    compensation, award of –
      amount of, determining, 11.66
      generally, 11.65
      reduction for failure to mitigate, 11.67
    contracting-out provisions, restrictions on, 11.73, 11.74
    detriment, following, 11.63, 11.64–11.67
    interpretation provisions, 11.77
    out of time matters, dealing with, 11.65
    well-founded complaint, declaration as to, 11.65
  failures of the system, parliamentary discussion as to, 11.90
  jurisdiction, prohibition on attempts to restrict, 11.74
  likely growth of cases under new legislation, 13.10
  reference to. *See* complaint to *above*

Injunction
  county court, proceedings in, 10.54

Injunction – *continued*
  criminal law, need for initial recourse to, before grant of, 10.53
  cross-undertaking as to damages, whether local authority required to offer, 10.55–10.61
  declaratory judgment, advisability of court refusing to give, 10.45
  exceptional nature of jurisdiction to seek, 10.44
  generally, 10.42
  jurisdiction of civil courts, 10.43, 10.44
  motion for interlocutory relief treated as trial of action itself, 10.53
  Order 14 proceedings resulting in, 10.53
  power of local authority to obtain, 10.46
  relator action, 10.57

Inspectors
  appointment of, 9.39
  obstructing –
    offence of, 9.47
    penalty for, 10.09, 10.10
  powers –
    conditions, subject to, 9.44
    entry onto premises, 9.45
    generally, 9.44–9.47
    measurement of premises, in connection with, 9.47
    production and inspection of records, as to, 9.46

Insurance company
  exemption from restrictions, 5.1

Internal floor area. *See* RELEVANT FLOOR AREA

Intoxicating liquor
  meaning, 5.6

Jewish exemption
  Board of Deputies of British Jews, applications to, 8.2, 8.3
  cancellation of notice –
    deemed cancellation, 8.16
    occupier's request, at, 8.15
    offence, following commission of, 8.17
  false statement in respect of –
    burden of proof, 10.13, 10.14
    nature of offence, 10.12
    penalty for, 10.12
  generally, 8.5–8.14
  historical background, 8.1–8.4
  local authority duties, 9.40–9.41
  local authority powers in connection with, 9.48
  non-Jewish bodies observing Jewish Sabbath, 8.9

Index

Jewish exemption – *continued*
  procedure for application to open –
    authority to grant certificate to accompany notice, 8.8
    cancellation of notice, deemed, 8.11
    certificate to accompany notice, 8.7
    change in occupier or composition of company/partnership, effect, 8.11
    generally, 8.6–8.14
    notice –
      precedent, Appendix 2
      service of, 8.6, 8.10
    partnership or company, in the case of, 8.6, 8.7, 8.11
    Shops Act 1950, s 53, shop registered under, 8.10
    simplification of, 8.5

Judicial review
  likelihood of success of application for, 9.33
  local authority's policy open to, 9.32
  proceedings by third parties, 9.36–9.38

Keep open clause
  assignment of lease, effect of subsequent, 7.5
  damages for breach of, 7.8–7.10
  generally, 7.1–7.10
  occupier not responsible for, where, 7.3
  protection for occupier, 7.3
  refusing to trade, damages for breach of covenant, 7.8
  sale of freehold interest, effect, 7.5
  shopping centre, shop in, 7.2, 7.6
  specific performance to enforce opening covenant, 7.8, 7.10
  sublease, affecting, 7.4
  Sunday, whether obliged to open on, 7.3

Keep Sunday Special Campaign
  earlier Bill, responsibility for defeat of, 1.16
  lobbying by, 1.16
  option for reform –
    amalgamation with RSAR option, 1.18
    publication of, 1.18

Large shop
  meaning–
    difficulties faced by prosecuting authorities, 3.15
    generally, 3.5
  blanket prohibition on opening, 4.2
  café within, whether subject to restrictions, 2.66, 4.20

Large shop – *continued*
  catering establishment within, 4.20–4.21
  Christmas Day, opening on, 4.18
  designation area, in, effect for loading and unloading purposes, 6.10–6.22
  Easter Sunday, opening on, 4.18
  effect of new legislation, generally, 4.1
  exceptions to ban on, 4.17
  exemption for, attempt to extend category of, 1.32
  illegal trading, nature of the offence, 4.4
  loading and unloading of lorries at. *See* LOADING AND UNLOADING
  non-retail customers, serving of, outside six-hour period, 4.3
  notice of opening, need to give. *See* NOTICE OF PROPOSED OPENING HOURS
  opening in connection with exemptions, whether need for notice to be given, 5.39
  opening hours, for serving retail customers, 2.45, 4.26
  opening small area of shop, in attempt to circumvent restrictions, 3.12
  permitted opening hours, following service of notice, 4.22
  public house within, whether subject to restrictions, 2.66
  register of large shops –
    contents, 9.7
    local authority's duty to maintain, 9.6
  relevant floor area, importance of, 3.4
  restaurant within, whether subject to restrictions, 2.66
  retail customers, opening for benefit of, 2.45, 4.26
  small shop within, whether subject to restrictions, 2.65
  take away food shop within, whether subject to restrictions, 2.66
  trading restrictions, 2.46

Launderette
  coin-operated –
    trading by, 4.4
    whether a shop, 2.15
  retail trade or business, whether constituting, 2.2
  shop, whether constituting, 2.30, 2.63, 5.1

Leaflets
  explanatory, provision of, whether a breach of restrictions, 4.7–4.8

Lease
  keep open clause in. *See* KEEP OPEN CLAUSE

127

Index

Lease – *continued*
rent review provisions, effect of new legislation on, 7.13
two-tier rental market arising, possibility of, 7.14
Leisure complexes
shops in, tabling of amendments to exempt, 1.32
Library
lending library, exclusion from definition of shop, 2.13
Licensed premises
brewers as occupiers where putting manager in as licensee, 10.28
Loading and unloading
environmental impact, 6.1
generally, 6.4
loading control area –
appeals in connection with, 6.29
designation –
consultation, need for, 6.6, 6.7
Council resolution, by, 6.9
difficulties, 6.5
effect, 6.10–6.22
generally, 6.5
notice of, publication, 6.8
procedure, 6.6
early deliveries –
application for, 6.16
causing undue annoyance to residents, 6.27
conditions, 6.19, 6.22
consent to application, 6.17
consultation, 6.18
fee for permission, 6.15
generally, 6.12, 6.13
information as to, 6.14
notice, publication of, 6.21
offences in connection with, 6.30–6.32
revocation of consent to, 6.24, 6.26–6.28
timetable for application, 6.20
variation of conditions, 6.24, 6.25
local authority's duties, 9.42
local authority's powers in connection with, 9.49
offences, 6.30–6.32
revocation of resolution, 6.23
local authority powers generally, 6.4
offence in relation to, 10.16–10.17
parliamentary discussions, 6.2, 6.3
Local authority
meaning, 9.2–9.4

Local authority – *continued*
duties –
enforcement duties. *See* enforcement duties *below*
generally, 9.5
inspectors, appointment of, 9.39
loading control areas, as to, 9.42
register of large shops, maintenance of, 9.6–9.7
enforcement duties –
acquiescence in breach, followed by attempt to enforce, 9.31, 9.32
action taken by third parties to secure compliance with statute, 9.33
advertisements, only responding to, 9.29, 9.30
best endeavours, need to use, 9.22
certain types of complaints only, responding to, 9.29, 9.30
components of, 9.15
criminal law, need to ascertain breach of, 10.52
difficulties face by authorities under former legislation, 9.10–9.13
discriminatory enforcement, problems of, 9.28
doubtful question of law involved, where, 9.24
enquiries prior to action, need to take, 9.17
expense involved, relevance of, 9.24, 9.25, 9.26
financial consequences need to have regard to, 9.24
generally, 9.8
importance of, 9.19
judicial guidance, 9.21–9.28
judicial review –
local authority's policy open to, 9.32
third parties, proceedings by, 9.36
lessening of, under new legislation, 9.14
limitations on, 9.9
mandamus, likelihood of authority being open to action for, 9.28
penalties, deterrence effect of, 10.52
pre-enforcement considerations, 10.49–10.61
previous legislation, comparison with, 9.10–9.12, 9.18, 9.20
principles to be adhered to, 10.50
proceedings to secure observance, taking, 9.20, 9.21–9.28

Index

Local authority – *continued*
  enforcement duties –
    selective enforcement policy, possible illegality of, 9.32
    shops opening but not classified as shops, 9.16
    unreasonableness of policy, consideration of, 9.34–9.35
    usual steps in securing observance, 9.23
    Wednesbury principles, application of, 9.34, 9.35
  injunction, right to seek, 10.46, 10.47, 10.48 *See also* INJUNCTION
  powers –
    generally, 9.43
    inspectors, of, 9.44–9.47
    Jewish exemption, in connection with, 9.48
    loading control areas, in connection with, 6.4, 9.49

Magistrates' court
  jurisdiction, 10.35
  proceedings in, 10.35–10.41
Mail order office
  shop, whether constituting, 2.63
Manager
  meaning 10.21
  offence committed by or due to fault of, 10.21n[1], 10.34
  prosecution of –
    for breach of restrictions, 10.22
    in substitution for the occupier, 10.25
Market
  building, operating from inside, 2.62
  indoors, whether constituting shop, 2.64
  outdoor stall, whether constituting shop, 2.63
  permanently covered, 2.57
  shop, whether constituting, 2.57, 2.63, 2.64
  temporary market, 2.57
  traders, exemption from legislative changes, 2.25
Maternity leave
  contract of employment, effect on, following return from, 11.83
  right to return to work following, 11.75
Medicinal product
  meaning, 5.12n[1]
Motor trade
  accessory shops –
    regulatory scheme proposals for, 1.23
    tabling of amendments to exempt, 1.32

Motor trade – *continued*
  car hire premises, whether subject to former Sunday trading restrictions, 2.8
  exposing cars for sale, 4.5
  goods priced etc and employee present, whether 'serving customers', 4.9, 4.10
  keep open clause in lease, 7.6
  motor accessory shop, exemption from restrictions, 5.25–5.29
  motor supply shop, relevance of nature of weekday trade, 5.35
  serving of customers, acts constituting, 4.5, 4.11
  supply shops, regulatory scheme proposals for, 1.23
Museum
  employment protection provisions –
    generally, 11.21
    gift shop worker, 11.21

Non-retail customers
  dangers of extending opening hours for sales to, 2.53
  legality of serving, outside six-hour period, 4.3
  shop opening for longer than six hours but restricting sales to, 2.53
Notice
  opting-in notice. *See* OPTING-IN NOTICE
  opting-out notice. *See* OPTING-OUT NOTICE
  precedents, Appendix 2
  proposed opening hours, of. *See* NOTICE OF PROPOSED OPENING HOURS
Notice of proposed opening hours
  cancellation –
    no intention of opening, where, 4.26
    occupier, by, 4.29
  contents, 4.22
  continuous period, reference to, 4.27
  date from which taking effect, 4.22
  effectiveness, importance of, 4.23
  fewer hours, effect of decision to open for, 4.26
  letter of explanation, advisability of sending, 4.31
  local authority, to, 4.22
  obligation to open, following service, 4.25
  occasional Sunday trading, for, 4.30
  occupier of large shop, by, 4.22

Index

Notice of proposed opening hours – *continued*
   part of permitted hours only, intention to open for, 4.28
   precedent, 4.31, Appendix 2
   public display, 4.32–4.34
   service, 4.22
   subsequent notice specifying different hours, 4.29
   timing of service, importance of, 4.23
   transitional provisions, 4.23
Nursery shop
   restrictions on trading, 5.34

Occupier
   meaning, 10.27, 10.28
   brewers putting manager in as licensee, where, 10.28
   company as, 10.28, 10.29
   incorrect occupier, prosecuting, 10.30
   offences by, identifying for purposes of prosecution, 10.27–10.30
   prosecution of, attempt to prosecute others following successful prosecution, 10.23
Off licence. *See also* PUBLIC HOUSE
   exemption from restrictions, 5.9–5.11
   relevance of nature of weekday trade, 5.35
   shop, whether constituting, 2.63
   supermarket, within, 5.9
   whether business 'wholly or mainly' the sale of intoxicating liquor, 5.10
   workers in, employment protection provisions, 11.19
Offences
   absolute nature of, 10.68
   duplicate offences, 10.25
   fines, 10.4, 10.10, 10.12
   generally, 4.24, 10.2
   Jewish exemption, false statement in respect of. *See* JEWISH EXEMPTION – false statement in respect of
   loading and unloading, in connection with, 6.30–6.32, 10.16–10.17
   obstructing an inspector, 9.47, 10.09, 10.10
   occupier, by, 10.23, 10.27–10.30
   opening of large shops on Sundays –
     burden of proof, 10.6, 10.8
     fines, 10.4, 10.7
     generally, 10.3–10.8
     notice, failure to exhibit, 10.7

Offences – *continued*
   penalties for, 10.31–10.32
   prosecution of directors for. *See* DIRECTORS – prosecution of
   third party, due to fault of, 10.33–10.34
Office
   shop, whether constituting, 2.63
Opening hours
   breach of restrictions –
     builder buying paint to paint own house, 2.51
   defences. *See* DEFENCES
   cancellation of notice following decision not to open, 4.26
   continuous period of opening, reference to, in notice, 4.27
   fewer hours than permitted in notice, shop opening for, 4.26
   non-retail customers, dangers of extending opening hours for sales to, 2.53
   notice of opening. *See* NOTICE OF PROPOSED OPENING HOURS
   permitted –
     following service of notice, 4.22
     no obligation to open during, 4.28
   retail customers, for serving, 2.45
   shop, meaning for purposes of –
     generally, 2.29–2.43
     inapplicability of earlier case law, 2.42
   six-hour period –
     advisability of limiting opening to, 2.52
     exceeding, non-retail customers, serving, 4.3
   'viewing only', stores open for, 4.6–4.9
Opted-out shop worker
   meaning, 11.42
   ceasing to be, 11.43
   opting-in notice, effect of giving, 11.43
   safeguarding of employment rights in absence of contract of employment, 11.42
Opting-in notice
   meaning 11.38
   contents, 11.38
   contract of employment –
     effect on, 11.83, 84
     variation following giving of, 11.85
   defects in legislation, 11.89
   effect of employee giving, 11.37
   opted-out worker giving, effect, 11.43
   precedent, 11.38, Appendix 2
   specific agreement to working on Sundays, advisability of avoiding, 11.39

Index

Opting-in notice – *continued*
two-step approach to, 11.38
Opting-out notice
contents, 11.40
contract of employment, effect on, 11.84, 11.85
detriment, right not to suffer after giving or proposing to give, 11.51
effective date, 11.41
opted-out shop worker. *See* OPTED-OUT SHOP WORKER
precedent, Appendix 2
service, 11.40
SHRC/USDAW undertakings as to, 11.88
variation of contract of employment following, 11.85
who may give, 11.41
Options for reform
KSSC/RSAR option, defeat of, 1.28, 31
publication of, 1.18
regulatory scheme, 1.21–1.23
SHRC option –
generally, 1.24–1.25
success of, 1.28, 1.31
total deregulation –
defeat of proposals for, 1.28, 1.31
effect of proposals for, 1.20
Out of town store
non-food sector, in, exemption from restrictions, 5.29

Pet shops
restrictions on trading, 5.34
tabling of amendments to exempt, 1.32
Pharmacy
exemption from restrictions, 5.12–5.13
in-store, open outside six-hour period, letter of explanation with notice, 4.31
opening in connection with exemptions, whether need for notice to be given, 5.39
registered, meaning, 5.12n[1]
sale of certain goods outside six-hour period, 5.13
Place. *See also* SHOP
examples of, 2.24n[1]
ice creams, depot and tricycle selling, 2.24n[1]
Plant hire shop
employment protection, 11.15
Port, shop, at
exemption from restrictions, 5.22–5.24

Post office
amendment of provisions relating to business of, 13.8
Premises
meaning –
difficulties in defining, 2.54
generally, 2.54–2.60
lack of statutory definition, 2.55
likely judicial approach to, 2.60
physical building, interpretation by reference to, 2.60
reference to other legislation, 2.56
entry powers of inspectors, 9.45
less than 280 square metres, 2.59
market stalls, 2.24
mobile retail outlets, 2.24
size of. *See also* LARGE SHOP
relevance to trading restrictions, 2.27
Premium pay
absence of provisions as to payment in new legislation, 11.89
SHRC/USDAW undertakings as to, 11.88
Private forecourt
covered by an awning, 2.56
roof and side walls, covered by, 2.56
shop, whether part of, 2.56
trading from, 2.56
Property law
considerations –
keep open clauses. *See* KEEP OPEN CLAUSE
service charges. *See* SERVICE CHARGES
Public house. *See also* OFF LICENCE
exemption from restrictions, 5.4, 5.7
large shop, within, whether subject to restrictions, 2.66
shop, whether constituting, 2.63, 5.7
workers in, exclusion from employment protection provisions, 11.18

Railway station
exemption for shop in, 5.18
whether problems likely to arise over meaning of railway station, 5.18
Records
advisability of keeping, 5.11
employer's duty to keep –
failure to keep, penalty for, 12.16
form of, 12.14, Appendix 2
generally 12.5, 12.7, 12.14
regulations as to, 12.15
statutory nature of, 12.14, Appendix 2
holiday records, prescribed form, Appendix 2

131

Index

Records – *continued*
  Inspectors' right to examine, 5.11
  prescribed form of employment and holiday records, Appendix 2
  production and inspection, 9.46
Redundancy
  employment protection provisions, 11.47–11.49
  opting-out notice period, for refusal to work before the end of, 11.48
  refusal to work on Sundays, for, 11.47
  unfair dismissal, constituting –
    opting-out notice, following employee giving or proposing to give, 11.49
    statutory right, following employee's assertion of, 11.68, 11.69
Register of large shops
  contents, 9.7
  local authority's duty to maintain, 9.6
Relevant floor area
  meaning, 3.7
  calculation –
    external areas of premises, exclusion from, 3.8
    generally, 3.7–3.18
    goods display areas, delineating, 3.14, 3.15
    hire, display area of goods for, classifying, 3.17
    marginal cases where layout changing from time to time, 3.11
    parts of floor area to be included, 3.9
    position for previous week, need to consider, 3.10–3.12
    serving of customers, delineating areas for, 3.13, 3.15
    where measurements should be taken from, 3.18
  large shop from small shop, importance in distinguishing, 3.4
  singles tennis court, equivalent to size of, 3.6
  size of, 3.5
Repair shop
  employment protection, 11.15
  retail trade or business, whether constituting, 2.2
  shop, whether constituting, 2.30, 2.63, 5.1
Restaurant
  exemption from restrictions, 5.4, 5.7
  large shop, within, whether subject to restrictions, 2.66, 4.20, 4.21
  shop, whether constituting, 2.63, 5.7

Restaurant – *continued*
  workers in, exclusion from employment protection provisions, 11.18
Retail
  meaning, 2.20–2.23
  generally, 2.44–2.53
Retail club
  employment protection provisions, applicability, 11.20, 11.22
  member purchasing goods for own use, 2.50
  shop, whether constituting, 2.46, 2.64
  trading restrictions, 2.46
Retail customer
  meaning, 2.45, 4.19
  opening hours for serving, 2.45
  sales outside opening hours, difficulties facing retailers, 2.47
Retail sale
  meaning, 2.45
  builder buying paint to paint own house, whether in breach of restrictions, 2.51
  six-hour opening period, outside, 2.51
Retail trade or business
  meaning –
    generally, 2.3
    inapplicability of earlier case law, 2.42
    judicial expansion of, 2.12
    retail, 2.20–2.23, 2.44–2.53
    retail business, 2.4
    retail trade (Home Office memoranda 1912, 1913), 2.7
  books and periodicals, lending for reward of, 2.11
  cleaning services, 2.14
  Costco. *See* COSTCO
  examples, 11.14
  place. *See* PLACE
  premises. *See* PREMISES
  retail clubs, 2.22, 2.23
  retail seller, meaning, 2.21
  sale of goods. *See* SALE OF GOODS
  trade, meaning, 2.4
Retailers for Shops Act Reform
  establishment, 1.16
  option for reform –
    amalgamation with KSSC option, 1.18
    publication of, 1.18

Sale of goods
  meaning, food and drink, for purposes of sale of, 5.5
  cars. *See* MOTOR TRADE
  generally, repeal of provisions as to, 13.2

Index

Sale of goods – *continued*
  holiday resort, at, repeal of provisions as to, 13.2
  intoxicating liquor, meaning, 5.6
  retail sale of, exclusions from meaning, 2.29
  turnover exceeding turnover for hire of goods, effect, 3.17
  under partial exemption order, repeal of provisions as to, 13.2
  whether business consisting wholly or mainly of, 2.33–2.35

Scotland
  hairdressers and barbers, regulation of business of, 13.7

Service charges
  failure of legislation to provide for, 7.11
  generally, 7.12

Service industry
  employment protection, 11.15

Serving of customers
  department store holding evening of hi-fi demonstration etc, 4.12–4.13
  explanatory leaflets, provision of, whether constituting, 4.7–4.8
  goods priced etc and employee present, 4.9, 4.10
  inspection of a car only, where garage selling motor accessories, 4.11
  judicial interpretation, 4.8–4.14
  promotion of sales, where intention is, 4.12–4.13
  trial run of a car, where garage selling motor accessories, 4.11
  use of signs denying the giving of personal service, 4.15

Shop
  meaning –
    evolution of, 2.5
    exemptions from, 2.63
    generally, 2.46, 12.8
    Home Office memoranda (1912, 1913), 2.7
    importance of defining, 2.26
    judicial interpretation, 2.4, 2.17
    Leasehold Property (Temporary Provisions) Act 1951, for purposes of, 2.36
    opening hours, for purposes of –
      generally, 2.28, 2.29–2.43
      inapplicability of earlier case law, 2.42
    rights of shop workers, for purposes of protecting, 2.28
    statutory, 2.3, 2.5, 2.6, 2.29, 11.13

Shop – *continued*
  meaning – *continued*
    test to determine amount of retail business, 2.37
    wrongful interpretation, possibility of, 2.19
  'about the business of a shop', meaning, 12.9–12.13
  'any premises', defined as, 2.55
  car boot sales, 2.57
  coin and stamp fair, 2.24n[1]
  coin-operated launderette, 2.15
  dairy used for storage not sale, 2.37
  dry-cleaning business, 2.16
  fairly permanent stall, 2.24n[1]
  ice creams, depot and tricycle selling, 2.24n[1]
  internal floor area, relevance, 2.56
  lending library, exclusion from definition, 2.13
  market, whether constituting, 2.57
  mechanical games, stalls containing, 2.24n[1]
  occasional market stall, 2.24n[1]
  regulation of opening hours, historical background, 2.6
  small shop. *See* SMALL SHOP
  trailer van, 2.24n[1]
  travel agents, whether a shop, 2.18
  uncovered market stall, 2.24n[1]
  within a shop, whether subject to restrictions, 2.65

Shop assistant
  meaning, 12.23
  break period, entitlement to, 12.22–12.24

Shop work
  meaning, 11.7

Shop worker
  meaning –
    question of fact, as, 11.11
    statutory definition, 11.6
  rights, SHRC/USDAW undertakings as to, 11.88
  types of, for employment protection purposes, 11.25

Shopping Hours Reform Council
  options for reform, new legislation, as background to, 2.25
  proposals for reform, 1.24–1.25
  undertakings with USDAW. *See* EMPLOYMENT PROTECTION – SHRC/USDAW undertakings

Shopping up time
  defence of, 10.63

133

Index

Small shop
  meaning, 3.5
  effect of new legislation, generally, 4.1
  exclusion from restrictions, 3.19
  within a large shop, whether subject to restrictions, 2.65
Souvenirs
  litigation as to meaning of, 1.7
  tee shirt with motif, 1.7
Statutory half-holiday
  meaning, 12.5
Store manager. *See* MANAGER
Sunday trading
  basic scheme of the Act, 3.1, 3.2
  employment protection. *See* EMPLOYMENT PROTECTION
  enforcement difficulties, where trader opening occasionally, 4.30
  European Court of Justice, reference to, 1.11, 1.12, 1.13
  exempt shops. *See* EXEMPT SHOPS
  existing position under Shops Act 1950, s 22... 12.5
  historical background –
    attempts to reform the law, 1.9, 1.10
    generally, 1.1–1.6, 1.15–1.33
    judicial criticism, 1.8
    litigation, 1.7, 1.11–1.14
    statutory changes, 2.11
  Jewish exemption. *See* JEWISH EXEMPTION
  local authority duties and powers. *See under* LOCAL AUTHORITY
  notice, need to give. *See* NOTICE OF PROPOSED OPENING HOURS
  options for reform. *See* OPTIONS FOR REFORM
  rearranging layout temporarily in order to circumvent restrictions, 3.12
  relevant floor area. *See* RELEVANT FLOOR AREA
  serving of customers. *See* SERVING OF CUSTOMERS
  shop worker protection. *See* EMPLOYMENT PROTECTION
  Shops Act 1950, Part I –
    effects of, 3.20, 3.21
    exemption from effects of, 3.22
  shops to which restrictions apply, 5.34
  statutory rights in relation to Sunday working, prescribed form describing, Appendix 2
  'viewing only', stores open for, 4.6–4.9

Sunday Trading Act
  children, repeal of provisions relating to street trade employment of, 13.4, 13.8
  clarity of provisions, 13.9
  commencement provisions, 1.36
  generally, 1.34–1.36, 13.1, 13.9–13.10
  prognosis, 13.9–13.10
  repeals under, 13.2–13.4, 13.8
  Royal Assent, to, 1.36
  Secretary of State's power to amend or repeal local Acts, 13.3
Sunday Trading Bill
  parliamentary procedure employed, 1.26–1.33
  publication of, 1.18
Supermarket. *See also* LARGE STORE
  keep open clause in lease, 7.6

Take away food shop
  exemption from restrictions, 5.4, 5.8
  food prepared to order, 5.8
  large shop, within, whether subject to restrictions, 2.66
  workers in, exclusion from employment protection provisions, 11.18
Telephone mail order business
  office premises, trading from, 2.58
  shop, whether premises constituting, 2.58
  six-hour period, conducted outside, 2.58
  trading restrictions, whether subject to, 2.58
Third party, offence due to fault of, 10.33–10.34
Trade
  meaning, 2.4
Trade customer
  methods used to identify, 2.48, 2.49
  sales to, as means of circumventing previous restrictions, 2.48
Travel agents
  employment protection, whether entitled to, 11.15
  retail trade or business, whether constituting, 2.2, 2.4
  shop, whether constituting, 2.18, 2.30, 2.63, 5.1

Unfair dismissal
  action for –
    age limits, absence of, 11.50
    qualifying period, absence of, 11.50
  constructive dismissal –
    event constituting, 12.2

Index

Unfair dismissal – *continued*
  constructive dismissal – *continued*
    protection under existing legislation, 12.6
  detriment amounting to, 11.52 *See also* EMPLOYMENT PROTECTION – detriment, employee's right not to suffer
  excessive hours, being forced to work, 12.2
  fixed term contract, failure to renew, 11.46
  opting-out notice, where worker giving or proposing to give, 11.45
  redundancy, by reason of, 11.49
  statutory right, following employee's assertion of, 11.68, 11.68, 11.69
Unitary authority
  meaning, 9.3
Unloading at large shops. *See* LOADING AND UNLOADING

Video hire shop
  employment protection, 11.15
  exemption from restrictions, 5.36–5.40
  opening in connection with exemptions, whether need for notice, 5.39
  retail trade or business, whether constituting, 2.2
  shop, whether constituting, 2.63
  whether subject to trading restrictions, 2.41
Viewing only
  stores open for –
    examples, 4.7–4.16

Viewing only – *continued*
  stores open for – *continued*
    generally, 4.6

Whole holiday, *meaning*, 12.5
Wholesaler
  employment protection provisions, applicability, 11.20, 11.22
  shop, whether constituting, 2.46, 2.64
  trading restrictions, 2.46
  wholesale trade, meaning, 11.22
Wholly or mainly
  meaning –
    judicial interpretation, 2.37–2.39
    parliamentary debates on, 2.33, 2.39
    planning condition case, used in, 2.38
    tests to decide, 2.40
    wide interpretation, possibility of, 2.40
  frequent use of expression by parliamentary draftsmen, 2.34
  sale of goods, whether business consisting wholly or mainly of, 2.33–2.35
  statute, example of use in, 2.36
Wine bar
  exemption from restrictions, 5.7
  shop, whether constituting, 2.63, 5.7
  workers in, exclusion from employment protection provisions, 11.18
Working hours
  lost, SHRC/USDAW undertakings as to, 11.88
Working week
  standard, SHRC/USDAW undertakings as to, 11.88

135